D1009713

To those who desire to better themselves.

Praise for George Eckes and *Six Sigma for Everyone*

"Long noted for his ability to simplify complex subjects and effectively move leaders and teams to action, George connects the dots in this new book. It is the 'help desk reference manual' to answer questions and light the path with advice on what needs to be done for effective Six Sigma implementation and what should be avoided. Without exception, this book should be within arms reach of anyone working in a Six Sigma environment. George summarizes his practical experience and advice on strategy, tactics, and the critical cultural acceptance dimension he pioneered. This book is written for the 'doers' in any position, function or organization serious about success."

Jay Williamson, Corporate Director of Quality,
Molex Incorporated

SIX SIGMA
FOR EVERYONE

GEORGE ECKES

John Wiley & Sons, Inc.

Copyright © 2003 by George Eckes. All rights reserved.

Published by John Wiley & Sons, Inc., Hoboken, New Jersey.
Published simultaneously in Canada.

No part of this publication may be reproduced, stored in a retrieval system, or transmitted in any form or by any means, electronic, mechanical, photocopying, recording, scanning, or otherwise, except as permitted under Section 107 or 108 of the 1976 United States Copyright Act, without either the prior written permission of the Publisher, or authorization through payment of the appropriate per-copy fee to the Copyright Clearance Center, Inc., 222 Rosewood Drive, Danvers, MA 01923, (978) 750-8400, fax (978) 750-4470, or on the Web at www.copyright.com. Requests to the Publisher for permission should be addressed to the Permissions Department, John Wiley & Sons, Inc., 111 River Street, Hoboken, NJ 07030, (201) 748-6011, fax (201) 748-6008, e-mail: permcoordinator@wiley.com.

Limit of Liability/Disclaimer of Warranty: While the publisher and author have used their best efforts in preparing this book, they make no representations or warranties with respect to the accuracy or completeness of the contents of this book and specifically disclaim any implied warranties of merchantability or fitness for a particular purpose. No warranty may be created or extended by sales representatives or written sales materials. The advice and strategies contained herein may not be suitable for your situation. The publisher is not engaged in rendering professional services, and you should consult a professional where appropriate. Neither the publisher nor author shall be liable for any loss of profit or any other commercial damages, including but not limited to special, incidental, consequential, or other damages.

For general information on our other products and services please contact our Customer Care Department within the United States at (800) 762-2974, outside the United States at (317) 572-3993 or fax (317) 572-4002.

Wiley also publishes its books in a variety of electronic formats. Some content that appears in print may not be available in electronic books. For more information about Wiley products, visit our Web site at www.wiley.com.

Library of Congress Cataloging-in-Publication Data:

Eckes, George, 1954–
    Six sigma for everyone / George Eckes.
        p.   cm.
    Includes bibliographical references and index.
    ISBN 0-471-28156-5 (PAPER : alk. paper)
    1. Quality control—Statistical methods.   2. Production
management—Statistical methods.   I. Title.
    TS156 .E283   2003
    658.5'62—dc21

                                    2002014909

Printed in the United States of America.

10   9   8   7   6   5   4   3

Preface

Six Sigma has been a popular management philosophy for years. Motorola first made Six Sigma popular in the 1980s. AlliedSignal embraced it in the early 1990s and then General Electric made it the most popular management philosophy in history.

Like anything that becomes popular, misconceptions abound relative to how to implement Six Sigma. Particularly since this management philosophy is based on facts and data being used to make decisions in the organization, a host of statisticians have developed new careers teaching and consulting in this discipline.

However, most statisticians are skilled in the theory of Six Sigma. To make Six Sigma a success in your organization, it must affect everyone in the organization. Thus, the title of our new book *Six Sigma for Everyone*.

Everyone in an organization must be involved and affected by Six Sigma, regardless of their position in the organization. Unlike the approaches many take that imply Six Sigma is some mystic set of skills available only to those with advanced college degrees, Six Sigma must be available to everyone in the organization, where certain skills are practiced by all.

Thus, the focus of this book is to *demysticize* this cutting edge management philosophy. At its foundation, Six Sigma is teaching everyone in the organization to become more effective and efficient. Unfortunately, most organizations are highly ineffective and inefficient. This means they have unhappy customers and waste considerable money because their processes do not run at optimum.

The path to becoming more effective and efficient using Six Sigma contains three components. The first component deals with the strategy of Six Sigma. The strategy of Six Sigma is called *Business Process Management*. This strategic component is the responsibility of executive management. Thus, if you hear your company has embraced Six Sigma it may be several months before you see the results of your management's initial work. To have you become acquainted with what your management has done to create the Business Process Management system, we review the key elements of Business Process Management and share an example with you in Chapter 2.

The second component of Six Sigma deals with the tactics of how project teams improve a broken process. It utilizes a methodology similar to the scientific method you learned in school. The *scientific method* refers to defining and measuring a problem, analyzing its root cause, and testing theories of improvement. In essence, this is the methodology used in Six Sigma to improve effectiveness and efficiency. In Chapter 3, we take you through the steps of improvement and what you can expect if you are placed on a Six Sigma project team.

In Chapter 4, we highlight the use of 10 common tools you can expect to use during your participation on a Six Sigma team. Instead of teaching you the theory of each tool we concentrate on how to use the tool and make your confidence grow.

Another key component of Six Sigma is the cultural one. In Chapter 5, we address 10 tools that your organization will use to make Six Sigma more than just a set of tactics.

Finally, everyone in the organization may have questions about how their organization will change under a Six Sigma management philosophy. In our sixth and final chapter, we address the 10 most common questions you might ask about your organization's effort to implement Six Sigma.

If your organization is embarking on a Six Sigma effort, you should congratulate yourself for being in an enlightened company. When implemented successfully, you will find being a part of this initiative challenging, exciting, and fun. *Six Sigma for Everyone* is your primer to making your journey easier to accomplish.

GEORGE ECKES

Acknowledgments

This book would not have been possible without the efforts of Matt Holt at John Wiley & Sons and the production work of Publications Development Company of Texas.

A special thanks to Debbie and Robyn for their ideas, suggestions, and proofreading. Thanks to my boys, Joe and Temo, for motivating me to be a better person. Finally, a very special thanks to the host of our clients who have taught us as we have taught them.

G.E.

Contents

CHAPTER 1

Why Has My Company Adopted Six Sigma?

What Can Six Sigma Do for You?

"Six Sigma is Greek to me."

—An Employee who just heard his company has
started a Six Sigma initiative.

So your company has just announced they have begun a Six Sigma quality initiative. You might be an experienced worker who has been through a quality initiative in the past. In all likelihood that experience was a bad one where you felt the time and money was wasted and negatively impacted your work life. Or you might be a new employee who wants to know what the excitement is all about.

You might have heard or read about Six Sigma in the newspaper as organization after organization has begun to adopt and implement this powerful management philosophy. What we want to do in this book is take away the mysticism of Six Sigma. In this first chapter, we answer your basic questions about Six Sigma. We provide you with a user-friendly definition of Six Sigma. We give you a brief history of Six Sigma and then explain why Six Sigma is different from other quality initiatives. We discuss what Six Sigma is going to do for your company and then complete the chapter with a discussion of what Six Sigma is going to do for you.

A Beginning Definition of Six Sigma

Companies exist to be profitable. Profitable companies provide jobs and pay taxes that benefit the community, state, and country where they make their products or provide their services. Making a profit is based on having customers who want your product or service. Wanting your product or service is just the beginning. Every customer has requirements regarding the product or service. Think of your most recent experience where you exchanged money for some product or service. Maybe that experience was ordering lunch at a fast food restaurant. You decide to use the drive-thru and order a cheeseburger, french fries, and a large Coke.

First, you get into a line of other cars where it takes almost 10 minutes to get to the order menu. When you place your order, you can hardly hear the order person through the speaker provided. You next drive your car around the drive-thru, pay your money to a person who, without a word or a smile, hands you a bag containing your order. You drive away, sticking your hand into the bag and pulling out a fry, hoping for a crisp, hot, salted snack on the way back to work. Instead, the fries are soggy and lukewarm. As you pull into your company's parking lot, you decide to play some music and eat your cheeseburger. Rather than the cheeseburger you ordered, you pull out a regular burger. You eat it anyway because you are hungry but decide the next time you will choose another place instead.

Your lunch experience shows that your customer satisfaction is more than just the exchange of a product or service for a fee. You exchanged your money for the product offered by the fast food restaurant but you were not happy. Your unhappiness was based on the restaurant not meeting your *requirements*. Requirements are those characteristics about your experience that determine whether you are happy or not. In this case, you probably had requirements about the accuracy of your order, the crispness and freshness of your french fries, and the time it took for your order to be filled. You might even have had a requirement about the courtesy of the person who handled your order. In this example, the restaurant did not meet your requirements.

In our fast food example, you didn't complain when your requirements weren't met. Instead you made the decision to take your business elsewhere. Think about the customers of your business. Are they happy with your products or services? Every business exists because it has customers. Every customer has a set of requirements. If you are meeting their requirements, you are being *effective*. If their requirements are not being met you are being *ineffective*. If you are ineffective and do nothing about it, soon you will be out of business.

Effectiveness through meeting (and preferably exceeding) requirements is only half the battle. Let's return to our fast food example for a moment. Let's suppose our fast food restaurant is committed to customer satisfaction. Suppose they widely advertise that if there is any customer dissatisfaction they will immediately replace the order free of charge and even deliver a new meal to wherever you are. Replacing your order and delivering it free to you would certainly increase customer satisfaction and make the restaurant a more effective organization. However, focusing merely on customer effectiveness would eventually mean they could go out of business. Why? Because to be a profitable business, an organization must also be *efficient*. Efficiency relates to the amount of resources consumed in being effective. Efficiency can be measured in time, cost, labor, or value. Thus, if the fast food restaurant has to hire more people as drivers, hire more people to cook burgers for a second or third time for the same customer, and pay for the materials to make these free burgers, they quickly will recognize that the cost of being totally focused on effectiveness without efficiency will result in an unprofitable situation. Since businesses exist to make a profit, being focused on the customer without also being focused on efficiency will not be a good business decision.

Six Sigma, at its basic level, is attempting to improve both *effectiveness and efficiency* at the same time. Again, let's return to our fast food restaurant. We have all seen the fast food restaurant with the golden arches that publicizes "Millions served." This concept of millions served will help us understand the basic concept of Six Sigma.

A technical measure of how many unhappy customer experiences per million opportunities is the concept behind *Six Sigma*. For example, if on any day McDonald's served one million customers, how many of them experienced what you did during your lunch experience? If only three (yes, three) customers were unhappy with their experience, then McDonald's achieved Six Sigma on that day. This is because Six Sigma is equivalent to only 3.4 bad customer experiences for every million opportunities.

Of course, do you think only 3.4 bad customer experiences at McDonalds occurred today? If 233 bad customer experiences occurred per million McDonald's customers then McDonald's would be a Five Sigma company. If 6,210 customers had experienced soggy french fries or an inaccurate order then McDonald's would be a Four Sigma company. If 66,807 McDonald's customers opened their lunch bag and found a Big Mac when they had ordered a Quarter Pounder, McDonald's would be a Three Sigma company.

Six Sigma is a measure of customer satisfaction that is near perfection. Most companies are at the two to three sigma level of performance–that means between 308,538 and 66,807 customer dissatisfaction occurrences per million customer contacts.

Companies that have a two to three sigma level of performance experience business problems. They don't make as much money as they should for their shareholders. Shareholders get mad and begin to take their money elsewhere. Management wants to increase profitability. They fear for their jobs and want to improve the "bottom line." Often, they think too much in the short term and begin to lay off employees. In the short term, the bottom line looks improved. Of course, the emphasis here is on the short term. With less people in the organization, there is more work for those who remain.

What management forgets by "downsizing" is that if they run a business that is neither effective nor efficient, things will only get worse with less people expected to work harder. Ultimately, businesses that operate by focusing on short-term profitability will result in long-term unprofitability.

In many companies, management believes that downsizing is a way to improve profitability. Since the 1980s, there have been attempts to change that approach. During the 1980s, some management improved profitability through downsizing. For example, the early 1980s showed an interest in Japanese manufacturing techniques. Some U.S. manufacturers mimicked these techniques. The early 1980s were marked by efforts like Statistical Process Control or Just in Time Manufacturing. While well intentioned, many of these efforts were ill fated from the beginning. Management attempted to use these efforts in the same way they used downsizing. That is, they attempted to use them as cost savings measures. The workforce saw these efforts for what they were, attempts to get more work out of less workers. This was particularly the case when these quality efforts were combined with downsizing. In addition, management only attempted to implement these initiatives as programs. What this meant was that the focus was almost exclusively on the tactics of improvement at the worker level with virtually no work done by management itself. For a company to truly become effective and efficient, it was necessary for a quality initiative to have a focus on changing how executives managed their business.

Six Sigma was started in the mid-1980s. Here was a quality initiative that had a significant role for management in its implementation. Started at Motorola but popularized in the 1990s by AlliedSignal and General Electric, Six Sigma was different than previous approaches to quality improvement.

With other quality approaches, management played little if any role other than approval of bringing in external consultants to train the workforce. With Six Sigma, the work begins with management. First, executives create the Process Management system. Before work is done that affects the average worker, management has already spent several months working on identifying and measuring the processes of their organization.

A *process* is defined as the series of steps and activities that take inputs provided by suppliers, add value and provide outputs for their customers. Six Sigma as a management philosophy instructs management to begin identifying the 20 or 30 most important processes in their business. Next management measures the current sigma performance of each of these processes. Many, if not all, of the processes will be operating at two to three sigma performance. Some processes may even be lower than two sigma. Once management has identified their processes and personally been involved in measurement of their current performance, they then identify the lowest performing processes that have the most direct impact on the company's business objectives. *Business objectives* are the five to seven most important goals a company establishes each year. Sometimes they are financially stated (like profits) but there are others like customer satisfaction or employee satisfaction.

Once the processes having the worst performance with the greatest impact to the business objectives are identified, project teams are formed. That's where the individual worker comes in. They will become part of a five to seven person team that will have the responsibility of improving the performance of the worst performing processes. These teams usually exist for four to six months. They are taught a series of tools and concepts (that we will cover in later chapters) to help them use their skills to improve sigma performance to achieve greater effectiveness and efficiency.

The History of Six Sigma

Motorola is where Six Sigma began. A highly skilled, confident, and trained engineer who knew statistics, Mikel Harry began to study the variations in the various processes within Motorola. He soon began to see that too much variation in any process resulted in poor customer satisfaction and ineffectiveness in meeting the customer requirements. While the concept of variation can be expressed statistically, it doesn't have to be complicated. Again, think of your lunch buying experience. Let's go back to our fast food restaurant where you are the customer. What if over the course of going there for lunch five days in a row, you experience the following waits in the drive-thru line measured in minutes from the time you join the line until you get your order filled:

- Monday (14 minutes),
- Tuesday (12 minutes),
- Wednesday (2 minutes),

- Thursday (24 minutes), and
- Friday (8 minutes).

The average wait in line for lunch this week is 12 minutes, (by the way, have you ever considered brown bagging it?). Yet, to say that you will typically wait 12 minutes in line doesn't describe the real situation. On Wednesday you waited only 2 minutes and on the very next day you waited 24 minutes. As my good friend and colleague Dave Schulenberg says, "Customers feel variation, not averages." Not having control over variation, this fast food restaurant is going to lose business, since you don't like the uncertainty of not knowing whether it is going to be a 2-minute wait or a 24-minute wait.

Mikel Harry recognized the importance of measuring variations in the various processes of Motorola. However, unlike other quality efforts that spent most time on measurement, Harry and others at Motorola acted on what processes produced the most variation. They applied a complete set of tools to reduce and control the variation in the poorly performing processes and greatly improved the effectiveness and efficiency of those processes. Not only did they improve those processes, they actively engaged their Chief Executive Officer, Bob Galvin, in their work. Soon, Galvin began to manage the variations in all of Motorola's processes and made Six Sigma the management philosophy in all he did.

In 1992, I was fortunate to hear Bob Galvin give a speech at the Juran Institute. While I was giving a speech on supplier management, I made sure to hear his keynote speech since I had spent time in the late 1980s working with several Motorola suppliers helping them begin to implement Six Sigma, albeit on a smaller scale than Motorola itself. After hearing that early November 1992 speech, I knew Six Sigma was going to be different. Never in my years of consulting had I observed an executive talking about a quality initiative. In the past, it was always other quality professionals talking about the craft of improvement, complaining accurately about the lack of management support.

If only other executives could have the passion of Bob Galvin, I thought that night. If only they could possess the type of commitment and involvement that Galvin was showing at Motorola, Six Sigma could become a true management revolution, moving management away from thinking of downsizing as their only approach to improving the bottom line.

I didn't have to wait long. At about the same time I was listening to Bob Galvin, he was having a series of private meetings with a man named Lawrence Bossidy. Bossidy had left General Electric in 1991 to take over a large conglomerate called AlliedSignal. Impatient but brilliant, he knew he wanted to make a major change in a once stalwart company that had fallen on hard times. Schooled by Jack Welch at General Electric, he wanted to place his own stamp on management at AlliedSignal and soon was in discussions with Bob Galvin about how he had helped Motorola improve their business performance.

Within months, Bossidy had generated significant improvements with Six Sigma, both improving effectiveness and efficiency through focusing on customer measures of effectiveness and generating greater efficiencies through both managing processes and chartering Six Sigma teams to improve performance. Within three years, AlliedSignal was saving literally millions of dollars and improving their reputation with customers while not resorting to cost cutting through downsizing or lay-offs.

Bossidy remained in close contact with his former mentor Jack Welch. Avid golfers, it was during a round of golf in early 1995 that Welch both complimented and inquired into Bossidy's turnaround at AlliedSignal. Always the competitor, Welch was intrigued by Bossidy's endorsement of Six Sigma and finally asked AlliedSignal to provide an overview of this management philosophy at his management training campus in Crotonville. With much anticipation, Bossidy relished the thought of returning to General Electric with a message of how he had changed an organization.

The summer meeting at Crotonville went well, with the General Electric audience encouraged by and complimentary toward this approach that AlliedSignal had used since the early 1990s. One problem was Welch's absence from the daylong session, though his absence was well excused. Welch had just gone through heart surgery and was recuperating at home. It wasn't long after his return that the buzz from the AlliedSignal meeting on Six Sigma made him a convert.

By the end of 1995, General Electric had decided to make Six Sigma a corporate-wide initiative. In his 20 years at the helm of General Electric, Welch claims to have had only three corporate-wide initiatives. [1] Again, like at Motorola and AlliedSignal, General Electric decided to make Six Sigma different than other programs that had been associated with quality. Six Sigma would have both the formal support and active involvement of management. It would be the way a company manages their business, not something to be foisted on the workforce as something extra to be done after they worked long hours making up for all the work left by those who had been laid off during downsizing.

As successful as Motorola and AlliedSignal were in their implementation of Six Sigma, General Electric is the organization that used Six Sigma most impressively to drive improvement in effectiveness and efficiency. In his autobiography, *Straight from the Gut,* Jack Welch described multiple successes that were generated through the application of Six Sigma. GE Plastics had wanted to obtain Sony's business for Lexan polycarbonates in the making of CD-ROMs and CDs. However, purity standards were very high, and General Electric was operating only at a 3.8 sigma level. After applying Six Sigma improvement methods, they went to a 5.7 sigma level and earned Sony's business. [2]

At GE Power Systems, rotors were cracking due to high vibration. A third of the 37 operating units had to have rotors replaced due to the high level of poor performance. Through application of Six Sigma methods, vibrations were reduced by 300 percent and, at the time of publication of Jack Welch's book, there had been no replacement of rotors. [3]

At General Electric Capital (where I did most of my General Electric Six Sigma consulting), customer response time dramatically improved in the mortgage business. At one point, getting a customer representative by phone averaged only 75 percent. After applying Six Sigma methods, this improved to over 99 percent.

---

[1] *Jack, Straight from the Gut,* Author Jack Welch with John A. Byrne, Warner Brothers Books, 2001.
[2] Ibid.
[3] Ibid.

Less than two years after the initial application of Six Sigma, General Electric had generated over $320 million in cost savings. By 1998, it had generated three quarters of a billion dollars in cost savings and anticipated over a billion dollars of cost savings by 1999.

What Can Six Sigma Do for Your Company and You?

In the past five years, literally hundreds of organizations have indicated their interest in making Six Sigma their management philosophy of choice. Of course, when anything becomes as popular as Six Sigma has become, problems can occur. Executives in many organizations who have a slash-and-burn mentality (quick profits through downsizing, remember them?) may now be trying to use Six Sigma in the same way. The *Wall Street Journal* has two or three articles on Six Sigma every week. While many of the businesses attempting to implement Six Sigma are well intentioned and want to implement Six Sigma properly just as General Electric did, there are also those impatient executives who now look on Six Sigma in the same way as they look on downsizing. This quick-fix approach to Six Sigma is a sure path to the same short-term results that hamper the organization in the long term.

There are a host of statisticians who now have printed business cards who claim they are Six Sigma consultants. Unfortunately, these consultants often only contribute to making the kind of bureaucracy that has a negative impact on effectiveness and efficiency.

Hopefully, your executives have made the right decision in hiring consultants who will help them implement this cutting edge management philosophy. By committing to Six Sigma, your management is displaying an enlightened attitude.

If they have, congratulate your management for being enlightened. What they have done by committing to Six Sigma is attempt to do several things. First, successful implementation of Six Sigma will result in improved effectiveness and efficiency in the first "wave" of projects in the first six to nine months of implementation. Of the 20 to 30 processes in an organization, usually 7 to 10 will be part of the first implementation efforts. Of those 7 to 10 projects, 4 to 7 will probably be successful. These first projects will help generate increased enthusiasm and momentum for future

Six Sigma activity within your company. We discuss in later chapters what your role will be whether in these first projects or in later projects.

In later months and years of Six Sigma implementation, you will notice other changes as well. First, while your reporting relationship within the organization may not change, you will be introduced to a group known as *process owners*. Process Owners are responsible for the management of processes within the organization. While the organization chart doesn't change, process owners take on informal responsibilities for the management of cross-functional, interdepartmental processes. These process owners may sponsor a team that is responsible for improving effectiveness and efficiency. These team sponsors are called *project champions*.

Your company is pursuing Six Sigma to change the way it does business. To their credit, your management team is trying to change the way it manages. They probably recognize the folly of previous attempts to increase profitability through downsizing. They believe that greater effectiveness and efficiency will bring improved profitability. Improved profitability means business growth. Growth means more jobs, not less. Increased growth can mean increased stock price that will benefit the executives and those who report to them as well as all other stakeholders.

Greater effectiveness and efficiency will mean a lot to you. First, it will mean greater job security. Second, it will mean learning new skills. These new skills will mean greater opportunities such as promotions in your current company. You may decide to take your new skills and market them to other companies. Even if you stay in your current job, you will find these new skills helpful. You will find using the tools of Six Sigma makes your job easier to do. Plus, working in processes that are effective and efficient means less stress and greater job enjoyment.

How This Book Is Written

The following chapters are written with you, the individual contributor, in mind. In Chapter 2, we expand the discussion started in this chapter and explain the strategic element of Six Sigma that is called *Business Process Management*. First, we describe what management has done to create Six Sigma as a true management philosophy in your company. This means using it as a strategic weapon. The *strategy* of Six Sigma is called *Business Process Management*. We address this strategy and provide an example.

In Chapter 3, we focus on the *tactics* of Six Sigma. In your role as an individual contributor, it will be likely that at some point in your professional life you will be put on a Six Sigma team. You will need to know what being on a team will mean to you. We will take you through the tactics of Six Sigma and give you practical ideas of what will be expected of you and what you can expect of others.

In Chapter 3, we spend more time on what will happen to you once you are on a Six Sigma team. Chapter 3 discusses the roles and responsibilities of a Six Sigma team and where you fit in. We take you through a high-level discussion of process improvement using a methodology of Defining, Measuring, Analyzing, Improving, and Controlling a process. Known by its initials DMAIC, we take you through this all-important methodology.

Chapter 4 focuses on the 10 basic tools you need to succeed on a project team. We do not cover the tools with statistical sophistication. Instead we discuss their importance to you and focus on what you need to use the quality tool properly. Among the tools we cover in Chapter 4 is the Customer Requirements Tree. This will help you determine what the customer's requirements are that ultimately lead to measures of effectiveness.

In Chapter 5, we address what will happen to your organization once Six Sigma becomes a true management philosophy. This cultural component is the key to making Six Sigma more than just a cost savings initiative. We discuss how an organization's systems and structures must change to embrace Six Sigma as a true cultural phenomenon through the use of 10 "soft" tools.

In Chapter 6, we discuss the 10 most common questions about Six Sigma and more importantly share with you the kind of answers that will strengthen your belief in Six Sigma.

Summary

Six Sigma is a popular management philosophy that is sweeping the globe. Its goal is to make an organization more effective and efficient. Effectiveness is the degree to which an organization meets and exceeds the needs and requirements of its customers. Efficiency is the resources consumed in achieving effectiveness.

Six Sigma is equivalent to no more than 3.4 bad customer experiences for every million customer opportunities. Most organizations operate at between Two to Three Sigma performance, which at best is nearly 70,000 bad customer experiences per million customer opportunities.

Six Sigma originated in the 1980s at Motorola. In the early 1990s, it migrated to AlliedSignal and in the mid-1990s, General Electric adopted it as their premier management philosophy.

KEY LEARNINGS

- Six Sigma is a management philosophy attempting to improve effectiveness and efficiency.

- Effectiveness is the degree to which an organization meets and exceeds the needs and requirements of their customers.

- Efficiency refers to the resources consumed in obtaining customer effectiveness.

- Efficiency usually refers to the time, cost, labor, or value involved in being effective.

- Six Sigma was first developed at Motorola.

- AlliedSignal was the second organization to be involved with Six Sigma.

- General Electric is the organization that made Six Sigma the most successful management philosophy in history.

- Unlike other quality initiatives that focused just on tools, Six Sigma is based on the active involvement it generates from management.

- Results from Six Sigma have not been paralleled by any other quality initiative.

CHAPTER 2

The Strategic Component of Six Sigma

In this chapter, we describe the strategic component of Six Sigma. First, we describe what management must do to create Six Sigma as a true management philosophy in your company; that is, using it as a strategic weapon. The *strategy* of Six Sigma is called *Business Process Management*. We address what it is and provide an example. While you may not be directly involved in the strategic creation of Six Sigma, your involvement in later project teams is a direct result of the creation of Six Sigma as a strategy in your organization. Learning what your management has done to create Six Sigma as a vibrant management philosophy will motivate you to see your place in the organization as Six Sigma is implemented.

The Strategy of Six Sigma

Quality initiatives have come and gone. You may have been part of one either in your current job or another place you have worked. Chances are these initiatives failed because their implementation involved jumping immediately into quality tactics without creating a strategy for the tactics to work.

A strategy may be defined as *a plan or method for obtaining some goal or result*. Unlike other quality initiatives, Six Sigma has a strategic component aimed at not only developing management's commitment to Six Sigma, but their active involvement.

One of the problems with previous quality initiatives is that the workforce soon came to see the quality activities as nothing more than a way for them to work harder. They saw how they had to change the way they worked and how they had to participate in teams, learning new concepts, but they didn't see management changing. In fact, with some quality initiatives the workforce soon saw that management would use the increased work to downsize the organization. When experts would analyze the results of a failed quality effort, high on the list of reasons behind the failure was the lack of management support.

Six Sigma is different because the work first and foremost begins with management. Management of any organization is responsible for the strategy of how work gets done (*a plan or method for obtaining some goal or result*). As a management strategy, Six Sigma is the plan or method for obtaining the goals or results of the business. To better understand how Six Sigma operates as a strategy, let's first put you in the position of executive management.

You have just been promoted as the chief executive officer of Fast Food Is Us. You inherit a company that has not been as profitable as it should be. You learn that any business must have a set of business objectives. Your board of directors has indicated you have five major strategic business objectives. They are:

1. Revenue.
2. Profit margin.
3. Customer satisfaction.
4. Growth.
5. Employee satisfaction.

As the chief executive officer, your success will be determined exclusively based on improvement of each of these objectives. Traditional management indicates that you have a group of vice presidents who manage a group of functions that hopefully drive achievement of these objectives. Figure 2.1 shows the traditional functions that have existed at Fast Food Is Us.

While you inherited the vice presidents, they are all hardworking and dedicated . . . to the achievement of their functional objectives. Each function has a set of objectives. For example, the vice president of food and beverage wants to make sure there is sufficient scheduling, delivery, and proper storage of food materials necessary to run the stores. The vice president of maintenance wants to ensure proper energy sources and back ups for each store. The operations vice president wants to ensure sufficient staffing. These functional goals and objectives are understandable but at times the functional objectives may be in conflict with the overall strategic objectives of the organization. For example, the vice president of food and beverage may want to hold unnecessary inventory so she isn't the cause of complaints regarding food. Holding inventory will impact revenue. Inventory may also impact customer satisfaction if freshness becomes an issue.

The focus of functional objectives denies the organization becoming world class. World class organizations have three major focus areas: being customer focused, process focused, and employee focused. As the preceding paragraph shows, your vice presidents want their functions to excel. As Figure 2.1 shows, the geometric shape of how most organizations are structured is vertical. However, customers don't go through our organization through a series of functions. Instead, recognize that customers go through your organization through a series of processes.

A *process* is a series of steps or activities that take inputs, add value, and produce an output. In our food example, our customers don't go through the food and beverage function. Instead, they go through a process that can be called the food delivery process. This process touches multiple functions (food and beverage, operations, and maintenance to name a few).

Thus, to create a Six Sigma strategy, it is the responsibility of management to identify the key processes of their organization, measure their effectiveness and efficiency, and initiate improvement of the worst performing processes.

Therefore, if you were the chief executive officer of Fast Food Is Us, your first responsibility would be to identify those processes.

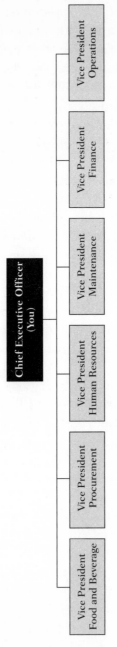

Figure 2.1 Fast Food Is Us—organizational chart.

18

Identifying these processes is best done with your current reports. Part of the goal of brainstorming the key processes of the organization is to educate management of the hazards of their current way of doing business. Thus, when the key managers get together in the same room and begin identifying processes, they are at the same time recognizing that there must be a better way to manage the business. Figure 2.2 shows a partial list of the key processes of a company like Fast Food Is Us.

Once management identifies their key processes, it is important for them to assign process ownership. In some cases, process owners will be current management. In other cases, a process owner might be taken from nonmanagement. The criteria for a process owner includes the following:

- A subject matter expert.
- Someone who experiences the gain if the process is working well and the pain if the process is working poorly.
- Someone who has respect among employees in preceding and subsequent processes.
- Someone with an aptitude for process thinking and improvement.

The process owner has the responsibility to acquire the key measures of performance for the processes they own. In Chapter 1, we said that Six Sigma improves the effectiveness and efficiency of the organization. To do this strategically, process owners are chartered with going out and first determining what the measures of effectiveness and efficiency are for the process (or processes) they own.

For example, let's say that Paula Pangborn is the process owner for food ordering. It would be Paula's responsibility to determine the measures of effectiveness and efficiency for food ordering. The first activity is to find out who is the customer of the food ordering process. Ultimately, the customer of the food ordering process is the external customer who orders a cheeseburger and fries. However, of far more importance are the most immediate customers of the food ordering process, which in this case are the food preparation employees. In this case, the process that follows the food ordering process is the food preparation process.

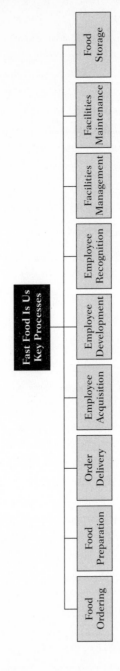

Figure 2.2 Fast Food Is Us—key processes.

Each process has customers. The customers of the food ordering process are the employees who transform the food into the final product for those who order the food.

Those in the food preparation process have requirements for their food. Therefore, the process owner of the food ordering process needs to first find out the requirements from these food preparation customers.

Finding out the requirements of the customer can be done through several methods. All of these methods have advantages and disadvantages. Figure 2.3 shows the major methods to find out about requirements from customers and a brief list of both advantages and disadvantages of each method.

Since each method of obtaining information has both advantages and disadvantages, it is suggested that multiple methods be

Method	Description	Advantages	Disadvantages
Interviews	Information obtained from customers either by telephone or in person.	• Detailed information • Follow up	• Expensive • Talent of the interviewer
Surveys	A set of written questions that is sent to selected customers to obtain information that can be formatted into data	• Objective data • Easy to interpret	• Poor response rate • Different answers based on type of questions
Focus groups	A collection of customers who answer questions from a facilitator	• Follow-up questions • Observing non-verbal behaviors	• Expensive • Skill of the facilitator
Observing the customer	Seeing the customer using your product or service	• Unfiltered information	• No follow up
Complaints	Information obtained while someone complains about a situation	• Opportunity to make amends	• Few people complain

Figure 2.3   Methods used to obtain customer requirements.

used. In the case of Paula Pangborn, the food ordering process owner, she first needs to seek out the process owner of the food preparation process. The work your organization is doing relative to Six Sigma strategy creation makes things a bit easier because the process owner of the food preparation process is the customer of the preceding process, food ordering.

Paula Pangborn sits down with Jim Badin of the food preparation process, along with several of his employees who also constitute the customers of food ordering.

This focus group was conducted on one day and information was obtained and prioritized. What Paula found out both confirmed and surprised her. The patterns in the responses she heard confirmed what she knew: Food delivery time was first and foremost their most important requirement. This she had suspected all along. In addition, accurate food quantity was confirmed as a customer requirement. What did surprise Paula was the additional requirement of food ordering. The surprise requirement was the *freshness* of the orders.

Suddenly Paula was seeing the beauty of Six Sigma and process thinking. Before the afternoon focus group, she had never thought about the importance of either the accuracy of her orders or the freshness of orders. Paula had been preoccupied with getting orders to the restaurants on time. Her experience taught her that she would be in the "hot seat" if there was not enough food in the restaurants. As a result, she often over ordered from her hamburger supplier in Nebraska, knowing full well that it would create an inventory problem for some of the stores. This over ordering kept Paula from hearing about shortages but created problems for the food storage process owner. Worst of all was the impact this over ordering had on the business as a whole. Over ordering and its impact on both inventory and ultimate spoilage negatively impacted multiple business objectives like revenue and profit margin. Only through seeing each link in the business as a series of suppliers and customers can an organization be considered truly high functioning.

Each process owner (who in many cases are higher level management) in the first months of creating the Six Sigma strategy validates the measures of effectiveness and efficiency for the process or processes they own. Once the process owner knows what are the more important measures for their process, they are expected to start collecting data on those measures. At its core, Six Sigma is managing with fact and data. Therefore, once it has been determined what is important to the customer, data must be collected to determine how well a particular process is performing against the customer's requirements.

In our food ordering process, Paula Pangborn collects data on three customer requirements:

1. Food delivery time.

2. Food order accuracy.

3. Food freshness.

For food delivery time, the food preparation group indicates that the target for delivery is on Tuesdays at 6:00 P.M. Further, the food preparation group indicates that a delivery is considered late if the delivery arrives at 8:00 P.M. and is considered too early if it arrives before 4:00 P.M. With the target and specifications (Target = 6:00 P.M. and the specifications being 8:00 P.M. and 4:00 P.M.), Paula Pangborn can now calculate the baseline sigma performance for her food delivery performance.

Figure 2.4 shows historical data from the last several months for deliveries. Note that Paula has taken the data and put it into a visual picture. This visual picture is called a frequency distribution check sheet, one of the more important Six Sigma tools we will cover in a later chapter.

This distribution of delivery performance for 22 previous deliveries shows that 11 of the 22 deliveries arrived *earlier* than the "window" of allowable time. Two deliveries arrived *later* than the "window" of allowable time. This window of allowable time

			X			
X		X	X	X		
X	X	X	X	X		
X	X	X	X	X	X	
X	X	X	X	X	X	
Previous days	12:00–2:00	2:01–4:00	4:01–6:00	6:01–8:00	8:01–10:00	Later days

Figure 2.4 Frequency distribution checksheet—food delivery times.

helps to define what is unacceptable to the customer. Anything that is unacceptable to the customer in terms of a product or service is considered a *defect*. Determining the number of defects is a critical part of calculating sigma performance. In this example, the 11 early deliveries and the 2 late deliveries are defects. Adding them together we have 13 total defects out of 22 total deliveries.

The easiest way to calculate sigma performance is defects per unit. The *unit* in this example is the food delivery. Here we had 22 deliveries (units). Dividing 13 defects by the number of units (13/22) equals 0.59. This means 59 percent of the deliveries are defects. If 59 percent of deliveries are bad, then 41 percent of the deliveries are considered acceptable by the customer (the number acceptable is called the yield). Figure 2.5 shows a sigma conversion chart for what would be the equivalent for a yield of 41 percent. A yield of 42.1 percent would equal a sigma of approximately 1.3. Therefore, a yield of 41 percent would be 1.29+ so we will round up and call the food service delivery baseline sigma 1.3. Similar sigma calculations are made for accuracy and freshness.

Most businesses in the United States operate between a two and three sigma performance. Operating at between two and three sigma in the eyes of the external customer will eventually spell your doom as an organization. In the previous example where the customer is internal, a 1.3 sigma may or may not be felt by the

Long-Term Yield	Process Sigma	Defects per 1,000,000
99.99966	6	3.4
99.98	5	233
99.4	4	6,210
93.3	3	66,807
84.1	2.5	158,655
69.1	2	308,538
50.0	1.5	500,000
46.0	1.4	539,828
42.1	1.3	579,260
38.2	1.2	617,911
34.5	1.1	655,422
30.9	1	691,462
15.9	0.5	841,345
6.7	0	933,193

Figure 2.5 Partial process Sigma conversion table.

external customer. Even if this process isn't directly felt by the external customer, they pay for the inefficiency of such a poor performing process.

In the creation of the Six Sigma strategy, each process owner is required to calculate the baseline performance of the processes they own. Once the key measures of each process have been validated by the appropriate customer(s), four to eight weeks later baseline sigma for each process should be completed. Once all the processes have had their baseline sigma performance calculated, a meeting is held where each process owner reports on their processes and their respective sigma performance.

Having facilitated many of these meetings, I can tell you they have a dramatic effect on those attending. Management gets to see, sometimes for the first time, how the entire organization is performing. It is a sobering day for many, particularly higher levels of management. The good news is that management suddenly sees why their higher level strategic business objectives are often not being met.

Why is this good news? If this happens in your organization, management will begin to see how they need to begin managing differently. Instead of just managing financial statements or managing by reducing staff to meet profit goals, management begins to see they need to start fixing the broken processes that constitute the totality of their organization. This eye-opening day is yet another reason why a Six Sigma initiative is different than previous efforts.

Summary

Six Sigma, unlike other quality initiatives that have come before it, is a management philosophy. As such, management must become actively involved in its application. The vehicle for this involvement is creating the strategy of Six Sigma called Business Process Management.

The steps involved in creating this strategy include identifying the key processes that affect the strategic business objectives of the organization. Once those processes have been identified, measures of effectiveness and efficiency need to be collected and validated. Once measures of effectiveness and efficiency are collected, the worst performing, highest impact processes are then targeted for improvement, which is the topic of our next chapter.

Key Learnings

- At its core, Six Sigma is a management philosophy. As such, it requires management's active involvement, not just their support.

- The vehicle for management's initial involvement with Six Sigma is to create the business process management system.

- The first step in the creation of business process management is to clarify and communicate the strategic business objectives of the organization.

- Once the strategic business objectives of the organization have been generated, management must identify the key processes of the organization and measure their current performance in terms of effectiveness and efficiency.

- The lowest performing, highest impact processes should be chosen for the tactics of Six Sigma.

CHAPTER 3

The Tactics of Six Sigma

Define, Measure, Analyze, Improve, and Control

In the first months of adopting Six Sigma as a management philosophy, the workforce may not see any differences in their organization. This is because, as we stated in Chapter 2, executive management is doing their job creating the strategy for Six Sigma to be more than a set of tools and techniques.

As we stated in Chapter 2, management must begin to identify the key processes of the organization and begin collecting data on current levels of effectiveness and efficiency measured in terms of current sigma performance. From these activities, certain processes will be identified as lower performing, higher impact (to the business objectives) projects.

These first projects are critical to the organization. For Six Sigma to be successful in your organization, the first "wave" of projects must be successful. Successful projects help the people in the organization see that Six Sigma works for them. Initially, there will be people who are skeptical about Six Sigma. These individuals will not be convinced of the importance of Six Sigma by referencing success stories elsewhere. They will be convinced that Six Sigma works only if they see it with their own eyes. Therefore, those individuals chosen to be part of the first wave of Six Sigma projects have an extra expectation, helping to convince those in the organization that Six Sigma will work.

In Chapter 2, we saw that the food ordering process had poor delivery sigma performance. It is typical in the first wave of projects for an organization to choose 7 to 10 projects for improvement based on impact to the business and current poor performance. In Chapter 3, we focus on two of the projects that Fast Food Is Us chose for their first wave of projects, the food delivery project and the drive-thru wait project.

The Concept behind Six Sigma Tactics

Working in any business environment can be a challenging endeavor. Most work environments are high-paced, energy draining experiences where everything has to be done at once. Unfortunately, these work environments end up being like a duck crossing a pond. On the surface, the duck looks like it is calmly traveling across the water. However, underneath the water line, the duck is furiously paddling.

What the Six Sigma tactics at the project level are trying to accomplish is greater effectiveness and efficiency. Whether it is the food ordering process or improving drive-thru speed and accuracy, what a group of five to eight individual contributors are trying to accomplish is to improve the process they live in.

Six Sigma tactics at the project level require you to participate on a team for four to six months. It requires you to spend about 20 percent of your time for work on the project. You will still be expected to get your normal work done. You shouldn't complain about the apparent "extra" work to be done being part of a Six Sigma team. You have been chosen to improve a process that is broken, that is, where you experience the difficulties of being ineffective and inefficient. Your management is devoting significant resources to the improvement of your work area. Treat this as an opportunity to make things better in your job, not as something extra to do.

To understand Six Sigma tactics conceptually, think of being back in school in science class. You may remember learning about the scientific method. The scientific method identifies some problem, measures the magnitude of that problem, determines why the problem exists, and generates a set of solutions to ensure that the problem goes away.

The tactics of Six Sigma and the project team you are on implements a set of tools and techniques associated with the scientific method. Figure 3.1 shows you the steps associated with the scientific method in Six Sigma language.

The Five Steps of Six Sigma Tactics

There are five high-level steps in the application of Six Sigma tactics. As can be seen in Figure 3.1, the first step is Define. In the Define step, the project team is formed, a charter is created, customers, their needs and requirements are determined and verified, and, finally, a high-level map of the current process is created.

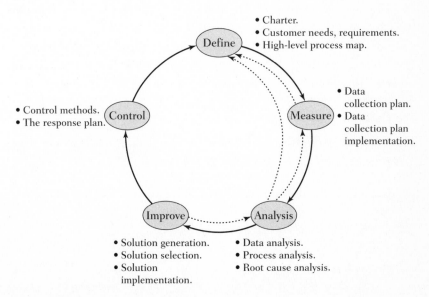

Figure 3.1   High-level DMAIC improvement methodology.

The second step of the application of Six Sigma tactics is Measure. It is in this second step that the current sigma performance is calculated, sometimes at a more detailed level than occurred at the strategic level of Six Sigma.

The third step in applying Six Sigma tactics is Analysis. During this step, the team analyzes data and the process itself, finally leading to determining the root causes of the poor sigma performance of the process.

The fourth step of applying Six Sigma tactics is Improve. In this step, the team generates and selects a set of solutions to improve sigma performance.

The fifth and last step is Control. Here a set of tools and techniques are applied to the newly improved process so that the improved sigma performance holds up over time.

As can be seen in Figure 3.1, the Define step of applying the tactics of Six Sigma includes three substeps. These substeps are called *tollgates*. Each of these tollgates indicates the specific work a project team must complete as they progress through each of the steps of Define, Measure, Analyze, Improve, and Control. These steps are shortened and known by their initials DMAIC.

The concept of the tollgate is relatively simple. If you ever have traveled on a turnpike, you know you pass through tollgates where you have to stop to pay a toll. Think of the tollgate of DMAIC in a similar fashion. Each tollgate should be seen as formal demarcations on the quality highway to improved sigma performance.

The Define Tollgates

There are three Define tollgates: Charter; Customers, their needs and requirements; and the High Level Process Map.

1. The Charter

The Charter is the collection of documents that provide purpose and motivation for a Six Sigma team to do its work. It includes:

- *The business case:* This is a sentence or two that describes why this project should be done, why it has priority over other projects, and indicates the strategic business objective(s) the project impacts.

- *The problem statement:* This is a short measurable statement about the problem. It should indicate how long the problem has been going on, be stated as specifically as possible, describe the gap between the current and desired state, describe the impact of the problem, and be stated in neutral terms with no blame, perceived solution(s) or root cause(s).

- *Project scope:* Scope refers to what the team should focus on but more importantly what the team should try to avoid. Six Sigma teams often fail when they don't clearly define what to work on and what not to work on.

- *Goals and objectives:* The goals and objectives are what the team should strive to achieve in the four to six months they exist. Typically, a first wave Six Sigma team should aim at improving the problem by 50 percent.

- *Milestones:* Milestones indicate to the team where they should be in the DMAIC process and when. For example, Define and Measure should take no more than 8 weeks of the project. Analysis should take no more than 6 weeks after Measure. Improvements should be implemented in the next 12 weeks. As a result of these milestones, the team should be ready to implement Control at the end of those 12 weeks devoted to Improvement implementation.

- *Roles and responsibilities of the project team:* There are several roles critical to the success of the Six Sigma team. First, there is the *Champion*. The Champion is usually the process owner who guides the project team strategically but will usually not be a full-time team member. They assist in picking the team, providing resources, and removing roadblocks that get in the way of the team doing its work. Second, there is the team leader, who is called the *Black Belt*. The Black Belt is responsible for the day-to-day activities associated with the team, from setting the team agendas, to keeping the team on track with meeting the specific responsibilities of DMAIC. If the team leader has organizational responsibilities other than being a team leader they are called a *Green Belt*. The *Master Black Belt* is equivalent to an internal consultant. They are not full-time members of the team but assist the team with the more technical aspects of their work on an as needed basis. The rest of the team are called team members and should be the subject matter experts who will conduct the actual work of the project.

Figure 3.2 shows the finished charter for the food ordering delivery project.

2. Customers, Their Needs and Requirements

Every project has customers. A customer is the recipient of the product or service of the process targeted for improvement. Every customer has a need (or multiple needs) from his or her supplier. For each need provided for, there are requirements for the need. As we stated in our previous chapter, the requirements are the characteristics of the need that determine whether the customer is happy with the product or service provided.

For the food ordering delivery project, the work of Paula Pangborn, the process owner, makes things easier for the project team. During her work at the strategic level, she was able to determine that the customer of the food ordering process was the food preparation process. Their need was a food order delivery. Their requirements were delivery time, accurate food quantity, and food freshness. In this example, the work of the process owner makes the work of the Six Sigma project team that much easier. Figure 3.3 shows a tool used commonly by project teams to help them identify the elements necessary to complete the second tollgate of Define, the customer requirements tree.

3. The High-Level Process Map

The third and last tollgate of Define is creation of the high-level process map. In Chapter 2, we defined a process as *"the series of steps and activities that take inputs, add value, and produce an output."* The critical last step in Define is to map out the process at a high level the way it exists today. There is an old saying, "A picture is worth a thousand words." That comment applies to the high-level process map. The symbols used in creating a process map are found in Figure 3.4.

To assist a team in creating their high-level process map, the team needs to be mindful of the suppliers, inputs, process, output,

Fast Food Is Us	Six Sigma Project Charter

Business Case (Connection to SBOs)

Food ordering delivery has experienced such variation that spoilage and inventory has increased. These negative effects of food delivery variation are negatively impacting revenue and profit margin.

Project Scope

IN	OUT
All domestic stores	Foreign stores
Food suppliers	Trucking firms

Goal and Objectives	Specialty Matter Experts
Reduce problems by 50%	

APPROVAL

Champion:
Date:

Team Leader:
Date:

Six Sigma Director:
Date:

(continued)

Figure 3.2 Completed charter template.

Problem Statement

Since June 14, 1999 Fast Food Is Us has experienced an average delivery time of 4:00 p.m. (versus the target of 6:00 p.m.) which has resulted in food spoilage, excessive inventory, and the inability for the food prep people to properly budget staff for off loads.

Expected Benefits	Target	Stretch
Total Savings	$ –	$ –

Milestones Start Date	Plan	Actual
Define	by November 2002	
Measure	by November 2002	
Analyze	by January 2003	
Improve	by April 2003	
Control	by May 2003	
Team:		
Champion	Paula Pangborn	
Team Leader	Jim Washington	
Master Black Belt	Frank O'Shaunessy	
Team Members	Role	Percent of Time
Anita Snite		
Robyn Haggar		
Jonas Brennan		
Brenda Faust		
Dustin Theisman		
Fiona Reckers		

Figure 3.2   *(Continued)*

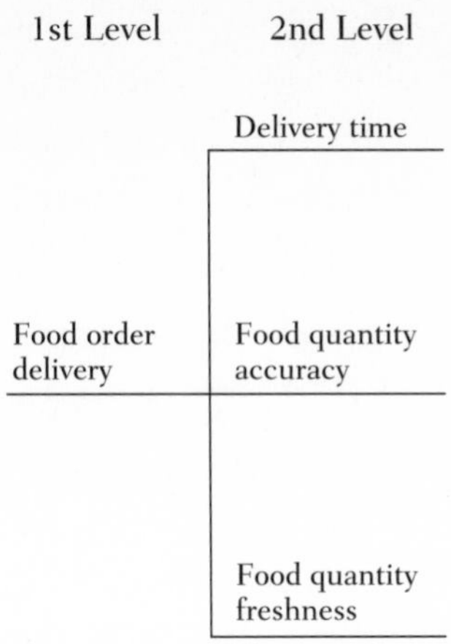

1st Level
2nd Level
Delivery time
Food order delivery
Food quantity accuracy
Food quantity freshness

Figure 3.3 Customer requirements tree—food preparation.

and customers (SIPOC). A high-level process map must be created in the following sequence:

1. Name the process (use nouns).
2. Establish the start and stop points of the process.
3. Determine the output(s) of the process (use nouns).
4. Determine the customer(s) of the process.
5. Determine the supplier(s) of the process.
6. Determine the input(s) of the process.
7. Agree on the five to seven high-level steps that occur between the start and stop points of the process (use action words like verbs and adjectives).

Start/stop of a process
Decision point
Step in the process
Direction in the process

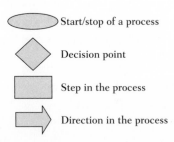

Figure 3.4 Process map symbols.

In the food ordering project, the team brainstorms what they think are the steps. Later the team is expected to validate what they brainstorm. Many times what the team thinks is occurring is not really the way the process is operating. Figure 3.5 shows the SIPOC for the food ordering delivery process.

The Measure Tollgates

There are two major tollgates in Measure, the creation of the data collection plan and the implementation of the data collection plan.

When a Six Sigma team is first formed, there is significant anxiety as they approach the Measure stage of DMAIC. There doesn't need to be this anxiety because the Measure stage of DMAIC is a relatively easy step.

It is important when approaching the Measure stage of DMAIC to remember that the Six Sigma team is trying to improve effectiveness and efficiency of the process they live in. Effectiveness applies to the output measures important to the customer and the effectiveness of your suppliers. The efficiency measures refer to what occurs inside the process whether it is the amount of time, cost, labor, or value occurring between the start and stop points in the process map.

Figure 3.6 shows the three areas where measurement should occur. These three areas center on the output measures important to the customer, the input measures important for you to do your job, and the actual process itself. You will note that these areas are reflected on the process map you created in Define.

1. Creation of the Data Collection Plan

The data collection plan has nine columns. Each column has an important role in helping the team calculate the last column, baseline sigma. Below are listed the columns and their definition:

- *What to measure:* In the first column of the data collection plan, the team should take the requirements determined in the Define stage of DMAIC and place them in this first column.

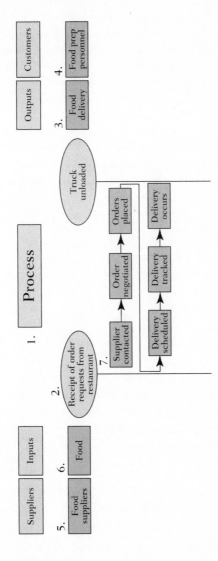

Figure 3.5 Process mapping example—food ordering delivery process.

Input Measures (Supplier Effectiveness)	Process Measures (Your Efficiency)	Output Measures (Your Effectiveness)
The key quality measures placed on your suppliers.	Measures of your process efficiency: • Cycle time • Cost • Value • Labor	Measures of how well you are meeting (and hopefully)/exceeding your customers requirements.

Figure 3.6   Areas requiring measurement.

- *The type of measure:* Teams make two major mistakes in data collection. The first type of mistake is not measuring enough and the second type of mistake is measuring too much. This second column determines if the project team will collect too much or too little data. Typically, there should be two or three output measures, one or two input measures, and at least one process measure. Using this as a guide, the project team can determine if they are collecting too much or too little data.

- *The type of data:* There are two types of data. The first type of data is discrete data. Discrete data is binary, off/on, good/bad, male/female. Continuous data refers to data that exists on a continuum such as height, weight, minutes, days, length, and so on. Continuous data is preferred over discrete data because it tells us more about a process. For example, feeling your child's forehead is discrete data collection. It certainly tells you whether your child has a fever or not but using a thermometer will tell you the magnitude of the fever and the ultimate course of action, whether it be child's aspirin or a trip to the emergency room.

- *Operational definitions:* The operational definition is a description of something where those affected have a common understanding such that all parties involved experience no ambiguity over what is being described. Coming up with operational definitions is important for the project team because data that is collected that goes counter to what people believe subjectively will not immediately be accepted. The data will be challenged. Getting agreement on what has been measured is an important step in getting people to agree about the results.

- *Targets/specifications:* The target measure is the customer's ideal performance of the product or service. In our food ordering delivery project, the target is 6:00 P.M. A specification is the least acceptable product or service in the eyes of the customer. In our food ordering delivery project, the specifications are 4:00 P.M. and 8:00 P.M.

- *Data collection forms:* There are two types of data collection forms. One is used for discrete data and the other used for continuous data. There are four steps to using a discrete data collection form:

  1. Determine what a defect is.
  2. Determine reason codes or categories of defects.
  3. Determine the time frame for data to be collected.
  4. Determine a grid for data to be collected.

Figure 3.7 is an example of a discrete data collection form taken from a grocery store giving reason codes for waits in line longer than 5 minutes.

For continuous data, the Six Sigma project team should use a frequency distribution check sheet. This type of check sheet tracks the number of occurrences for a given event for each measurement or series of measurements put into what are called *cells.*

Item	Frequency	Comments
Price check	142	
No money	14	
No bagger	33	
Register out of tape	44	
Forgot item	12	
Override	86	Manager assistance needed.
Wrong item	52	
Miscellaneous	8	

Figure 3.7 Discrete data collection form.

Figure 3.8 is an example of a frequency distribution check-sheet taken from the work of Paula Pangborn when she collected data on food ordering delivery times.

- *Sampling:* Sampling is the process of taking only a proportion of the total population of available data, when measuring the entire population would either be too expensive or take too much time. To ensure that sampling is done correctly, the sample must be representative of the larger population and be taken randomly.

  A representative sample is one where the sample represents the larger population. For example, if we wanted to sample all the voters in California we wouldn't want to just sample men and not women. We would also want a cross section of voters that would address such issues as age. For example, the sample should not just take young or old voters but a sample along a spectrum of age. We would also want a representative sample based on affluence (not just poor or rich but a representative sample of poor, middle class, affluent, and the rich). The sample needs to be representative not equal. For example, in the case of the poor, they tend not to vote as much as other income groups so they will not have as many represented in the sample. Geographical location would be another factor in assuring a representative sample.

  A random sample ensures that any one sample has an equal likelihood of being taken. For example, on your CD player there may be a random button. What this means is that by hitting this button, song number five has an equal

			X			
X		X	X	X		
X	X	X	X	X		
X	X	X	X	X	X	
X	X	X	X	X	X	
Previous days	12:00–2:00	2:01–4:00	4:01–6:00	6:01–8:00	8:01–10:00	Later days

Figure 3.8 Frequency distribution checksheet—food delivery times.

likelihood of being played first as song number two or song number nine and so on. Taking a random sample is important so that the Six Sigma project team does not introduce a bias in the sample. An example of a bias due to a nonrandom sample in the food ordering project would be if the team only samples trucking firms that begin with the letter A or B. What if there were delivery problems with the Zenith Trucking Company? If there were a nonrandom sample where the team only sampled the first trucking firms filed alphabetically, the Zenith Trucking Company would never have a chance to be sampled.

For all intent and purpose, this is the completion of the first tollgate. Calculation of the baseline sigma constitutes the next tollgate, implementation of the Data Collection Plan.

2. Implementation of the Data Collection Plan

The second tollgate is taking the Data Collection Plan and implementing the plan to generate the baseline sigma:

- *Calculating baseline sigma:* There are several methods to calculate baseline sigma. The easiest way is to determine what a unit, defect, and opportunity is for your project. In our food ordering project, a unit is a food order delivery, and a defect can be created by a delivery being either too early or too late. However, at the project level, we want to go deeper into calculating sigma. The food ordering team should also determine the sigma for the other two customer requirements: accuracy of food order quantity and freshness. The team is free to calculate three separate sigma calculations or combine them into one calculation. If they determine that they want to calculate one sigma, they would calculate what is called *defects per million opportunities* (some teams call this sigma the "mother" sigma). They would determine how many early or late deliveries they have, how many problems they have had with freshness, and how many times they were inaccurate with food order quantities. An example follows:

Food order unit:	A delivery.
Food order defects:	Delivery time either too early or too late.
	Food order quantity inaccurate.
	Food order not fresh.
Number of opportunities:	3 (one for each of the above ways to generate a defect).

The food ordering delivery project team examines 50 deliveries and finds out the following:

> Delivery time either too early or too late (13).
>
> Food order quantity inaccurate (3).
>
> Food order not fresh (0).

To then calculate the defects per million opportunities we would implement the following equation:

$$\frac{\text{Number of defects}}{\text{Number of units} \times \text{Number of opportunities}} \times 1{,}000{,}000$$

In this example, there are 16 defects, 50 units (deliveries), and three opportunities. Therefore, we calculate:

$$\frac{16}{50 \times 3}$$

$0.107 \times 1{,}000{,}000 = 106{,}666.7$ defects per million opportunities.

We then use the chart in the Appendix that shows that 106,666.7 defects per million opportunities is equivalent to a sigma performance of between 2.7 and 2.8.

The Analysis Tollgates

There are three Analysis tollgates: Data Analysis, Process Analysis, and Root Cause Analysis.

Analysis is seen by many as the most important step in the DMAIC methodology. This is due to the fact that many project teams have preconceived notions of what to do to improve a process. After measurement, they will want to jump right to improve. An example may prove helpful.

In my first Six Sigma book, I told the story of the new Denver International Airport. Stapleton, the old Denver airport, was plagued with delays. Excited politicians didn't bother conducting analysis that would determine why there were delays. If they had, they would have discovered that limited parallel runways were the root cause behind the delays at Stapleton. Without that analysis, they immediately jumped to the solution they desired, a new airport. Unfortunately, this new airport was very expensive and inconvenient to local users.

Six Sigma project teams are not unlike the politicians in Denver. Many teams will want to jump to improving the process without verifying why the problem exists. Therefore, it is vitally important for teams to conduct analysis of the data and/or process, ultimately conducting Root Cause Analysis if they are to be successful as a team.

1. Data Analysis

Data collected during the measure phase of DMAIC needs to be analyzed, particularly if the team has a goal to improve the effectiveness of some customer's requirement. The type of data analysis is dependent on the type of data collected in the measure phase of DMAIC, discrete or continuous.

Discrete Data Analysis

Think of variation in any process as being the enemy to the Six Sigma team trying to improve sigma performance. There is an old saying: "It's easier to fight an enemy we can see." Therefore, we want to create statistical pictures of the enemy we call *variation*. When data collected in the measure phase of DMAIC is discrete in nature, the most common statistical tools we use are the Pareto chart and the pie chart.

Discrete Data Analysis: The Pareto Chart

The Pareto chart is named after an economist, Vilfredo Pareto, who mathematically proved in the sixteenth century that 80 percent of the world's wealth was controlled by 20 percent of the population. This concept is popularly called the 80–20 rule. For example, 80 percent of your day is spent on 20 percent of what your job description entails.

If we return to the discrete data collection chart used in the grocery example, we would take the discrete data collection check sheet and transform the data into a Pareto chart (Figure 3.9).

It is clear that between the price check (which was calculated at contributing 36.3 percent of reasons for waits in the checkout line of greater than five minutes) and the price override (which accounted for 22.0 percent of the reasons) that only two of the reason codes account for nearly 60 percent of the defects in this process. While this isn't quite 80 percent, you should clearly see the power of organizing discrete data into a Pareto chart.

The beauty of the Pareto chart is that it will be much easier for the Six Sigma project team to reduce the largest contributor (price check) than it would be to work on the lesser contributors like no money or forgotten item.

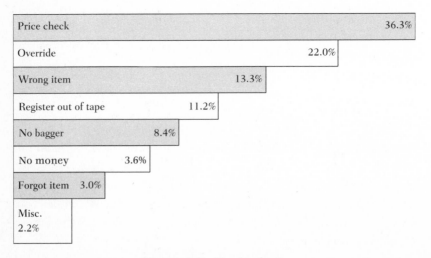

Figure 3.9 Pareto chart.

DISCRETE DATA ANALYSIS: THE PIE CHART

Another discrete data analysis tool is the pie chart. Similar to a Pareto chart, the pie chart divides reason codes for defects into different categories. Like the Pareto chart, the pie chart separates the vital few from the useful many. In Figure 3.10, you see a pie chart dividing the percentages of defects for an injection molding Six Sigma project. Note that each defect was categorized into one of several reason codes.

The pie chart is analyzed in a similar fashion to the Pareto chart. We can see that warpage is the biggest issue related to defects for this injection molding project.

CONTINUOUS DATA ANALYSIS

Continuous data that is collected in the Measure phase of the DMAIC project is collected using the frequency distribution check sheet. As we indicated earlier, it is preferred that the team collect continuous data because it tells us much more about what is going on in a process than discrete data. For example, earlier in this chapter we reviewed one advantage of continuous data: It tells the team the magnitude of the problem facing them, as we highlighted in the fever example.

CONTINUOUS DATA ANALYSIS: THE FREQUENCY
DISTRIBUTION CHECK SHEET

Another advantage of continuous data is that it tells the Six Sigma project team about the factors that influence the performance of

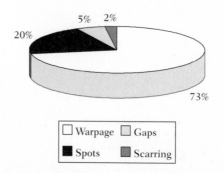

Figure 3.10 Injection molding pie chart.

the process. In any process there are six major factors affecting the performance of the process. They are:

1. Machines in the process.

2. Materials used in the process.

3. Methods in the process.

4. Mother Nature or the environment.

5. Measurement itself.

6. The people.

When no one of these 5Ms and 1P, as they are casually referred to, are having an undue influence on the process, the continuous data is "bell" shaped (because the distribution resembles a bell), with most of the measures in the middle and the rest tailing out in either direction.

We now turn to another initial project at Fast Food Is Us to highlight the next steps in DMAIC. In Figure 3.11, we see an example taken from the food order delivery process of Fast Food Is Us. This project has as its goal to improve drive-thru wait time without impacting the accuracy of orders.

This is the average wait in line for the drive-thru window for one of the franchises. The measure is from the time a car stops in

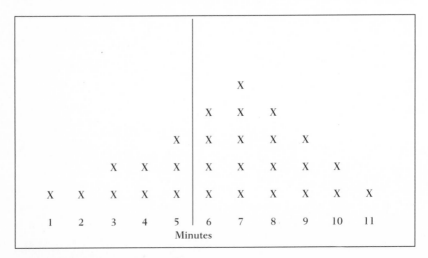

Figure 3.11 Frequency distribution checksheet—order delivery process—common cause variation.

line to the time the employee hands the customer their order. The vertical line indicates the maximum allowed time before a customer considers the wait time to be too long (five minutes).

As we can see, most of the measures are in the middle and fewer tail off in each direction. By using continuous data, we have evidence that no one of the 5Ms or 1P have had an undue influence on the drive-thru process. The technical name when no one factor has an undue influence in the data is *common cause* variation, because the variation is caused by a common set of variables, the 5Ms and 1P.

However, as shown in Figure 3.11, we have a problem with the drive-thru process because most of the measures extend past the allowable time customers want to wait in line. Therefore, this process may have common cause variation but it is a process with low sigma performance. Unfortunately, management who don't understand common cause variation will react the wrong way when customers start to complain about the wait at this drive-thru line.

In all likelihood, you have worked for a manager who didn't understand common cause variation. Maybe you work for one now. If that manager who was responsible for the drive-thru started having problems with customer complaints, what would he or she likely do? Unfortunately, they would probably tell the employees (the people in the 5Ms and 1P) to start working harder or faster.

The problem with this quick fix solution is that the data says the people are no more responsible for the performance of the process than the 5Ms. The picture of the data showing common cause variation indicates a process problem which management is responsible for, not the people in that process. To focus on one of the Ms or P when you have common cause variation is both inefficient and not too smart. It is particularly problematic when management focuses on people, telling them to work harder or faster in the face of common cause variation.

In our drive-thru example, if employees work faster they may make the process worse by filling orders incorrectly (remember our story from Chapter 1), taking the wrong order, cooking the order wrong, or even dropping the food and having to recook the meal; all of which results in *longer lines*.

Now examine Figure 3.12. Here is an example where most of the values don't trail off into either direction from the middle. This is an example of a nonrandom or *special cause* process. It is called special cause because one or more of the 5Ms or 1P have some undue or special influence on the process. Still, it would be wrong to focus on the P. That is because less than 5 to 15 percent of the time special cause is due to people. In manufacturing processes, the machine is the predominant undue influence when special cause variation is present and the method is the predominant undue influence in the service industry.

In both examples, we see the advantage of analyzing continuous data to tell us what is going on in the process even if we hadn't been there watching the process ourselves. It also shows the importance of management understanding common cause versus special cause variation, since knowing the difference is important for later corrective action.

CONTINUOUS DATA ANALYSIS: THE RUN CHART

Another continuous data analysis tool is the run chart. A run chart tracks some value over time allowing us to see if there are any shifts or trends in the data. Figure 3.13 shows a run chart for the drive-thru process during another period of time.

										X	
								X	X		
							X	X	X		
						X	X	X	X		
					X	X	X	X		X	
				X	X	X	X	X		X	
		X	X	X	X	X	X	X	X		
X	X	X	X	X	X	X	X	X	X		
1	2	3	4	5	6	7	8	9	10	11	
					Minutes						

Figure 3.12 Frequency distribution checksheet—order delivery process—special cause variation.

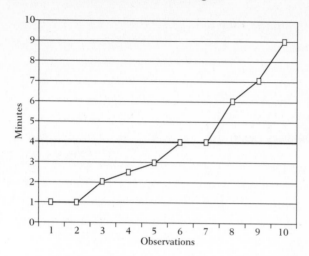

Figure 3.13 Run chart delivery time.

The horizontal line indicates the average wait for the drive-thru line is 3.95 or four minutes. However, by tracking the data over time using a run chart, we can see an increasing trend in the data. A trend is defined as seven points in a row or more in increasing or decreasing order. A trend of seven points or more is evidence of special cause variation. Therefore, once again, this drive-thru manager should be aware of a special cause problem and investigate the 5Ms and 1P. Just like the frequency distribution example of special cause variation (Figure 3.12), the focus should be on the method and not simply urging people to work harder or faster. A trend is present when one or more of the 5Ms or 1P is having an undue influence on the process. Since this is a service process, it is likely the method should be investigated.

2. Process Analysis

For project teams who have goals more focused on improving efficiency, process analysis is critical to the success of the project. Process analysis includes creating a more detailed process map and analyzing the more detailed map for where the greatest inefficiencies exist.

PROCESS ANALYSIS: SUBPROCESS MAPPING

Earlier in this chapter we showed the high-level process map steps that the food ordering Six Sigma team established. They were:

- Suppliers contacted.
- Order negotiated.
- Order placed.
- Delivery scheduled.
- Delivery tracked.
- Delivery occurred.

For purposes of process analysis, subprocess mapping refers to taking one or more high-level process step from the original high-level map and "drilling down" to the five to seven steps below the high level. Often these steps will reveal inefficient, non-value-added steps that later the team should attempt to change or even remove. Figure 3.14 takes one of the steps (Order negotiated) and tracks the subprocess steps.

PROCESS ANALYSIS: THE NATURE OF WORK

Once the subprocess map has been created and validated by the project team, they need to analyze the map for where non-value-added steps are located.

A subprocess step is considered to add value when the step in the process meets the following criteria:

- The customer of the step in the process considers it important.
- There is a physical change to the product or service.
- Its done right the first time.

The Six Sigma team must analyze the subprocess map to see if every step meets all three criteria. If any step does not meet all three criteria, the step is considered non-value-added. Each non-value-added step then must be categorized into one of the following types of non-value-added activities:

- *Internal failure:* Steps that must be done more than the first time.
- *External failure:* Failures in the process detected by the customer.
- *Delays:* Waits in the process.

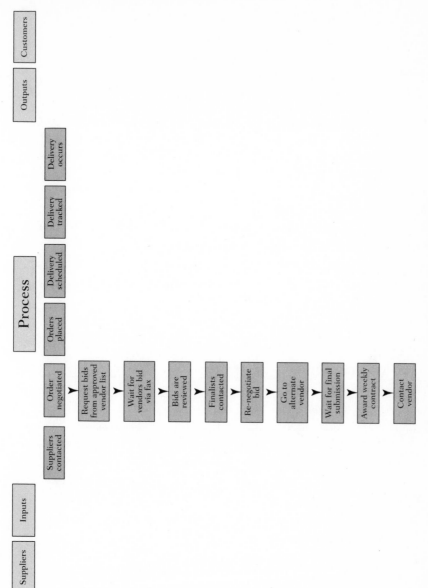

Figure 3.14 Order negotiation subprocess.

- *Control/inspection:* Steps in the process that verify previous work has been done correctly.

- *Preparation/set-up:* Steps in the process that prepare a following step to be done.

- *Moves:* Steps that move a product or element in service from one place to another.

- *Value enabling:* A non-value-added step in the process that would not be targeted for improvement because it is necessary for the functioning of the organization.

For each subprocess step that is considered non-value-added, the project team must determine which of the aforementioned non-value-added types it is. Figure 3.15 shows the subprocess steps as either adding value or not. If the step does not add value, the type of non-value-added activity is indicated and in the last column the amount of time each subprocess step takes is indicated.

While there are nine steps, only five add value. Moreover, there are 196 hours of activities and only 28 hours is considered

Subprocess Step	Value Added	Nonvalue Type	Time (Hours)
Request bids from vendor	X		24
Wait for vendor's bid via fax		X Wait	48
Bids are reviewed	X		1
Finalists contacted	X		1
Renegotiate bid		X Internal failure	24
Go to alternative vendor		X Preparation/setup	48
Wait for final submission		X Wait	48
Award weekly contract	X		1
Contact vendor	X		1
Total			196

Figure 3.15   Order negotiation—subprocess value/non-value analysis.

value-added time. This is equivalent to only 14 percent of the subprocess steps adding value.

There are four types of non-value-added steps in this process. Two waits (totaling 96 hours of the subprocess), an internal failure (which accounts for 24 hours of the subprocess), and a prep/set up (which accounts for 48 hours of the subprocess).

MICRO PROBLEM STATEMENTS: THE LAST STEP IN DATA AND PROCESS ANALYSIS

Whether you are conducting data analysis or process analysis, the last step before entering root causation is to create one or more microproblem statements. The microproblem statement is actually phrased in the form of a question that begins with the word, "Why . . ."

Microproblem statements allow the project team to become more specific with regard to the problem they are trying to impact. Microproblem statements come from either data analysis or process analysis.

For example, in our drive-thru data, the microproblem statement could be derived from the trend we discussed earlier. The micro-problem statement could be stated as:

Why is there a trend toward longer wait times in the drive-thru?

Similarly, process analysis done by the Six Sigma project team may also produce a microproblem statement. From process analysis previously discussed in this chapter, a microproblem statement could be stated as:

Why are there so many waits in this process?

If the project team analyzes both data and the process itself, it is common for the Six Sigma project team to generate at least two microproblem statements. It is strongly advised that the project team only create two or three microproblem statements. Any more than that usually means the project team has not done a sufficient job in analyzing the data or the process.

3. Root Cause Analysis

The third and most important tollgate of Analysis is *root cause analysis*. As stated previously, Six Sigma project team members will likely have their own pet theories about how to improve the process they work in. While we want to tap into the expertise of the team members, it is also true that a Six Sigma project team must let "data lead the way." Many teams ignore going through root cause analysis, jumping prematurely to the Improve phase of DMAIC.

When done properly, the root cause analysis section of the Six Sigma project team's work is the key ingredient to project success.

THE THREE STEPS TO ROOT CAUSE ANALYSIS

Project teams must go through three important steps for root cause analysis to be done properly. They are:

1. *The open step*: During this phase of root cause analysis, the project team brainstorms all the possible explanations for current sigma performance.
2. *The narrow step*: During this phase, the project team narrows the list of possible explanations for current sigma performance.
3. *The close step*: During this phase, the project team validates the narrowed list of explanations that explain sigma performance.

ROOT CAUSE ANALYSIS: THE OPEN STEP

A simple formula to help the team through root causation is:

$$Y = f(x)$$

The Y in this formula refers to the problem associated with the microproblem statement. Therefore, taking the microproblem statements above we are trying to find out what process variables (the xs) explain the microproblem statement.

In the open phase of root causation, the Six Sigma project team brainstorms all the possible xs that could explain the problem stated in the microproblem statement (the Y).

The team uses the concept of brainstorming to complete this task. Good brainstorming includes the following concepts:

- All ideas are documented.

- The team generates ideas not discussion.

- No evaluation of ideas occurs during the "open" step.

- Everyone on the team participates. (Silent brainstorming using one idea per Post-it note ensures all members participate and generates many ideas.)

The preferred tool used by Six Sigma project teams to accomplish brainstorming is the cause-effect diagram that is seen in Figure 3.16.

There were two major microproblem statements completed by the project team. We now take one of them and show a partial cause-effect diagram in Figure 3.17 for the drive-thru project team.

ROOT CAUSE ANALYSIS: THE NARROW STEP

Once the project team has brainstormed as many ideas as the team members have, it is time to narrow the larger list of xs that could explain the microproblem statement (the Y).

In the open phase of root cause analysis, the project team is using their technical expertise and experience. This remains the case during the narrowing phase of root causation. First, the project team gathers together similar ideas that were brainstormed by different team members. They also ask for clarification on ideas not understood and do not evaluate or criticize the ideas during this phase. Many times this will narrow the larger list from brainstorming.

Next, the project team votes on the more likely xs. Voting in this situation is not decision making. It is simply a way to narrow the list to the more likely root causes. Each team member should be given a certain number of votes (three to five is customary) and be allowed to distribute them among the root causes they believe explain the micro problem statement. This voting method typically narrows the list of possible root causes to 7 to 10, though sometimes there are more. Even if a root cause doesn't receive enough votes to be among the narrowed list, its okay to add one or two that a team member feels strongly about.

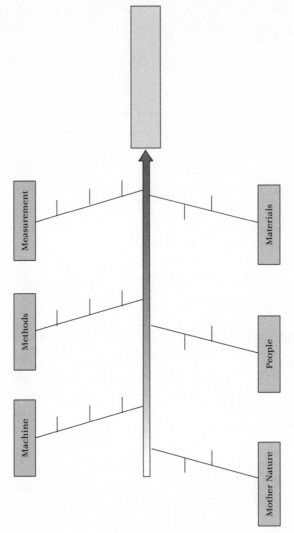

Figure 3.16 The cause-and-effect diagram template.

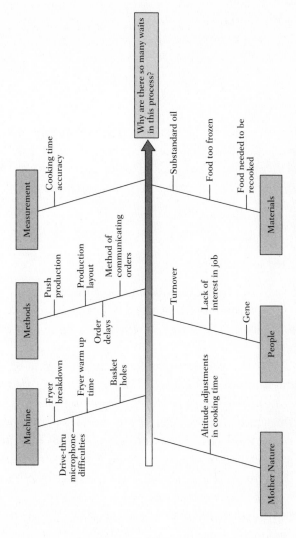

Figure 3.17 The cause-and-effect diagram completed.

In the drive-thru project, the team uses the multivote technique and arrives at the following narrowed list of *x*s to explain *Y* (Why are there so many waits in the drive-thru process?):

Y = Waits, which are a function of:
x_1 = Push production
x_2 = Production lay-out
x_3 = Method of communication
x_4 = Food needs to be recooked
x_5 = Turn over

ROOT CAUSE ANALYSIS: THE CLOSE STEP

The close step of root causation is the most important step in this tollgate. It is in the close step that team members' theories (sometimes called hypotheses) are tested with data. Testing the narrowed list of potential root causes can be done through:

- Basic data collection.

- Scatter analysis.

- Designed experiments.

Each of these methods are attempting to validate the $Y = f(x)$ formula. It is recommended that the project team use basic data collection methods first, if they can, since they typically are easier tools to use.

For the drive-thru project team, they first take one of their *x*s (turnover) and attempt to do research on whether this drive-thru's turnover is any better or worse than competitors who have efficient drive-thru times. A member of the project team does comparisons of over 10 other fast food outlets and finds out that their turnover is no better nor any worse than competitors who have good drive-thru times. Thus, through the process of elimination, this *x* is no longer under consideration.

Next, the project team does a scatter diagram on drive-thru time and recooking frequency. A scatter diagram plots some *x* that can be measured continuously and measures the corresponding performance of *Y*.

Figure 3.18 shows the relationship of pressure on an accelerator pedal (the *x*) when it is measured from low pressure to high

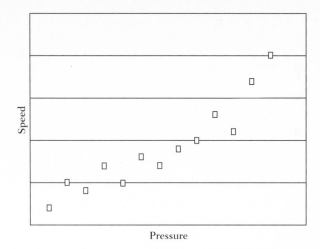

Figure 3.18 Scatter diagram—speed versus pressure—validation of root causation.

pressure and the corresponding measure of Y (speed of the vehicle). Clearly, you can see that as x goes from low to high Y goes from low to high. This is called a positive correlation. When x goes from low to high and Y goes from high to low then you have a negative correlation. There are other interpretations possible from no correlation to special patterns.

Figure 3.19 shows the data of frequency of recooking orders and drive-thru time. You can see that the relationship is strongly correlated.

During a project team meeting shortly after this scatter diagram was shown, a project team member indicated that maybe the recooking frequency that led to drive-thru waits was due to another x still under consideration of the team, which was method of communication. When the team clarified this x, it became misunderstanding the order through the microphone system. The team set up a simple one-factor experiment where five different fast food workers wrote down an order and then made their order as taken through the drive-thru microphone four times each. These 20 tests revealed that 50 percent of the time the order was taken wrong because of the garbled message. The data from this experiment validated the x of method of communication.

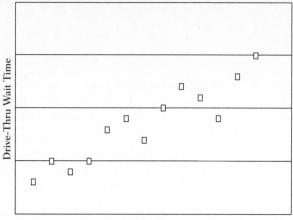

Figure 3.19 Scatter diagram—drive-thru wait time versus recooking frequency—validation of root causation.

It is rare when only one x explains Y in total. Therefore, the team conducted two additional experiments, changing the "pull method" of production to a "push method" of making orders only when requested rather than building inventory. (Wendy's is noted for this procedure.) In combination with changing the production layout, these last two xs were validated as major contributors to the drive-thru delays. Therefore, the validated formula that came out of root causation for drive-thru delays looked as follows:

Drive-thru delays is a function of method of communication (x_1) + Production method (x_2) + Recooking (x_3) + Layout (x_4).

With the root causation validated for their project, the team could now go on to the Improve phase of DMAIC.

The Improve Tollgate

If the project team does a thorough job in the root causation phase of Analysis, the Improve phase of DMAIC can be quick, easy, and satisfying work. There are two Improve tollgates, generating solutions and selecting solutions.

Let's take the work done by the drive-thru team and see how easy it can be to progress through Improve. Figure 3.20 shows

Root Cause (xs)	Solution
x_1 Method of communication	New microphone system with written verification of order.
x_2 Production method	Changing to a "pull" order of production similar to Wendy's made to order.
x_3 Recooking	Since recooking was validated as related to the method of communication, the solution for x_1 would apply here.
x_4 Layout	A new layout was created that fit with the new "pull" system based on the flow of work in each restaurant.

Figure 3.20 Validated root causes and proposed solution chart.

each of the four validated root causes and the proposed solution(s) generated by the drive-thru Six Sigma project team.

It is recommended that when implementing solutions, the project team prioritizes the solutions and implements them one at a time or in groups, immediately following implementation of the solutions with a recalculation of sigma. This should be done because many times the goals and objectives of the project team may be achieved without implementing all the proposed solutions.

The Control Tollgate

There are two major tollgates to the last phase of DMAIC. They are:

1. Determining the technical method of control.
2. Creating the response plan.

1. Determining the Technical Method of Control

Once improvement has occurred, it is important to make sure that the solutions "stick" over time. The method of technical control is based on how much throughput goes through the new process and how much standardization the new process has. Figure 3.21 shows a matrix to determine what technical tool is used based on the level of throughput and standardization, and how often Eckes & Associates sees this type of situation. In the case of

High standardization Low throughput 15%	High standardization High throughput 80%
Low standardization Low throughput <1%	Low standardization High throughput 5%

Figure 3.21   Process throughput-standardization matrix.

the drive-thru process, throughput and standardization is determined by the project team to be "high."

   Thus, the drive-thru process will use a type of statistical control
chart to ensure that drive-thru time remains consistent, predictable, and repeatable. Figure 3.22 is an example of the drive-thru
control chart. The control charts dotted lines are called the upper
and lower control limits. These control limits are not the specification of the customers; instead, they indicate when the process is no
longer operating consistently. This would prompt the employees in
the process to examine what could have changed that would make
the process no longer operate in a consistent manner. Usually, it is
because one of the improvements implemented by the team is not
being followed. When a control chart goes "out of control" it is an
example of "special cause" variation. Again, focus should not be on

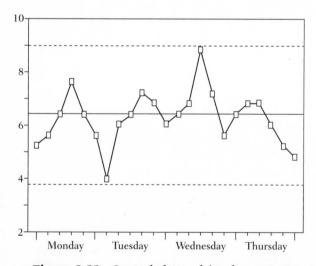

Figure 3.22   Control chart—drive-thru process.

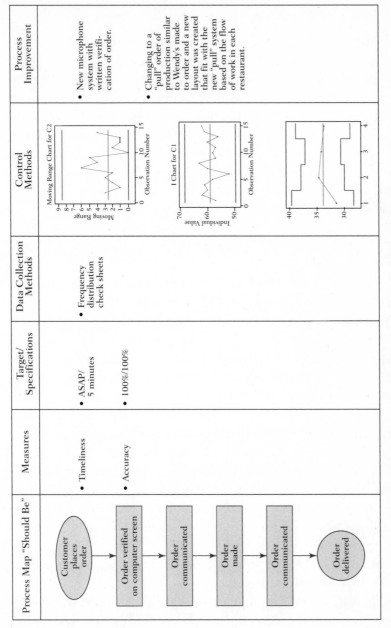

The table contains the following columns:

Process Map "Should Be"	Measures	Target/Specifications	Data Collection Methods	Control Methods	Process Improvement
Customer places order → Order verified on computer screen → Order communicated → Order made → Order communicated → Order delivered	• Timeliness • Accuracy	• ASAP/5 minutes • 100%/100%	• Frequency distribution check sheets	Moving Range Chart for C2; I Chart for C1; control chart plots	• New microphone system with written verification of order. • Changing to a "pull" order of production similar to Wendy's made to order and a new layout was created that fit with the new "pull" system based on the flow of work in each restaurant.

Figure 3.23 Process improvement hand-off—the response plan.

the people in the process since the odds are against people being the "special cause."

2. Creation of the Response Plan

The second and final tollgate of Control is the creation of the response plan. Figure 3.23 shows the response plan for the drive-thru process improvement team. The response plan is similar in appearance to the data collection plan. It chronicles the new process map the team creates as a result of their improvements (called the should-be map), the most important measures for the new process, the specifications and targets as verified by the customers of the process, what data collection forms are used, the control methods chosen by the team (in this process, control charts), and the most notable process improvements.

Summary

In this chapter, we addressed the DMAIC improvement methodology that drives improvement of effectiveness and efficiency on selected projects targeted for improvement.

We addressed how to create the project charter, define the customer, their needs and requirements, and how to create a high-level map of the current process. These steps constitute the Define phase of DMAIC.

Next we addressed how to create and implement a data collection plan where ultimately the project team calculates baseline sigma performance. This is the Measure phase of DMAIC.

We stressed the importance of the Analysis phase of DMAIC, where the project team analyzes the data they collected, the process in greater detail, and most importantly, brainstorms and validates a set of process variables that they believe are the root causes for current sigma performance.

Improve is the next step in DMAIC. If the team does a good job in Analysis, this step should be relatively easy.

Finally, in the Control phase of DMAIC, the team determines how to technically control the newly improved process and creates a response plan to ensure the new process maintains the improved sigma performance.

KEY LEARNINGS

- The tactics of Six Sigma are very much like the scientific method learned in elementary school.

- The scientific method is based on defining a problem, measuring the impact of the problem, determining root causes, and forming and testing hypotheses.

- The tactics of Six Sigma are made up of five steps: Define, Measure, Analyze, Improve, and Control.

- The five steps of tactical Six Sigma are sometimes known by their initials DMAIC.

- Each step in DMAIC has a series of substeps known as tollgates.

- The tollgates of Define include creating the team's charter, identifying the customers of the process, their needs and requirements, and creating a high-level map of the process.

- The tollgates of Measure include creation of the data collection plan and implementing that plan.

- The tollgates of Analysis include analyzing the data, analyzing the process, and analyzing the root causes for current sigma performance.

- Analysis is the most important step to implement in project success.

- The tollgates of Improve include generating and selecting solutions.

- The Control tollgates include choosing and implementing a form of technical control over the new process and creating a Response Plan.

CHAPTER 4

10 Technical Tools to Master While on a Six Sigma Team

In Chapter 3, we reviewed the steps a team goes through as they attempt to improve the sigma performance of a process.

Chapter 4 addresses the 10 most important technical tools a Six Sigma team member needs to master as they progress through the DMAIC methodology.

While these tools are considered technical in nature, most of them are relatively easy to learn and apply. They are covered in the order they are used in the DMAIC methodology.

Tool #1 The Critical to Quality (CTQ) Tree

The critical to quality tree is used in the second tollgate of the Define phase of DMAIC. It is used to brainstorm and validate the needs and requirements of the customer of the process targeted for improvement.

The steps in creating a CTQ tree are as follows:

- Identify the customer of the process targeted for improvement. A customer is the recipient of the product or service of the process.

- Identify the need of the customer, that is either the product or service desired by the customer.

- Identify the first level of requirements of the need, that is, some characteristic of the need that determines whether the customer is happy with the need.

- Drill down to more detailed level(s) of the requirement if necessary. Some requirements of the customer dictate greater specificity. If so, the tree will need to be created in greater detail.

Figure 4.1 shows an example of a CTQ tree for a health care provider where the customer of the patient registration process is the patient. The need of the patient is to be registered. However, you can also see that there are requirements of the patient that will determine whether the patient has been satisfactorily registered.

Figure 4.1   Health care provider CTQ tree.

Keys to Using This Tool

- Always start with the need of the customer.

- State the need as a noun with no adjectives to describe it.

- Keep moving left to right until you describe how to measure the detailed requirements. If you have described a measurement, you have gone to far (e.g., a requirement could be speed or timeliness, but if you put it in minutes you have described a measurement).

- Once you have started a branch for the tree, all those branches should be a greater detail of the preceding requirement, *not* a new requirement.

Tool #2 The Process Map

During the Define phase, the project team creates the first of several process maps. A process map is a picture of the current steps in the process targeted for improvement.

A process map has five major categories of work from the identification of the suppliers of the process, the inputs the suppliers provide, the name of the process, the output of the process, and the customers of the process. Each of these steps is summarized as SIPOC to indicate to the team the steps that must be conducted to complete a process map.

There are four stages of process mapping. The first stage is what the project team creates during the Define stage of project work. It is the *high-level* process map because the project team focuses in on the five to seven highest level steps in the current process. Sometimes there will be less than five or more than seven but most teams should strive to have five to seven.

The second step in process mapping occurs during the Analysis stage. Here, the original high-level process map is created in more detail. This second type of process map is called the *subprocess* map. The third type of process map is created during the Improve stage of DMAIC. This map is the improved map of what the new process should be. Ergo, it is called the *should-be map*. Finally, the fourth type of process map is the *could-be* map, usually generated in the Design for Six Sigma application. (Design for Six Sigma is not addressed in this book.)

Figure 4.2 shows an example of a high-level process map for a hospital lab test ordering process. In addition, we have also talked about the subprocess map created in the Analysis stage of DMAIC. Figure 4.3 shows the same hospital lab test ordering process with one of the high-level steps drilled down in greater detail showing the hospital lab test subprocess map.

Keys to Using This Tool

- Don't rush to the creation of the should-be map, this occurs in the Improve stage of DMAIC.

- Capture all of the steps as they actually occur in the process, not the way you would like to see the steps in the process.

- Use verbs or adjectives to describe steps in the process.

- Use unqualified nouns to describe the output and inputs of the process.

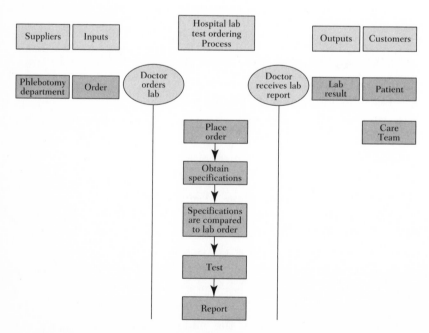

Figure 4.2 Hospital lab test ordering—high-level process map.

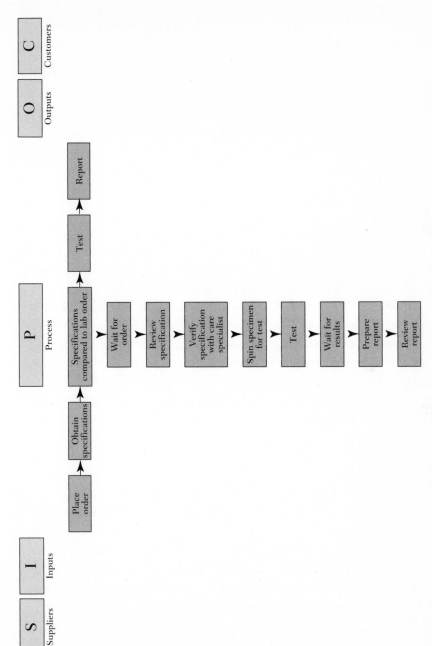

Figure 4.3 Subprocess map–hospital lab test ordering process.

71

- To verify any map, do two things. Talk to the people in the process and follow the product or service through the process. For example, in the case shown, the project team should follow a lab order from beginning to end.

- Make sure to capture both easily seen and *invisible* steps. Invisible steps are the waits or moves of the product or service being mapped.

- Don't map the best or worst case map, map what is representative of how the process normally works.

Tool #3 The Histogram

During the Analysis stage of DMAIC, the project team will review data collected during the Measure stage of DMAIC. It is often suggested that the data be organized into graphs or charts to more easily understand what the data is saying about the process. As W. Edwards Deming, the noted quality guru said, "Variation in any process is the enemy and it's easier to fight an enemy you can see."

Data is of two types. Discrete data is either/or, go/no-go, pass/fail type data while the other type of data exists on a continuum and is called continuous data (time, height, etc.). For continuous data, the best tool to use is the *histogram,* a graphical display of the number of times a given event is seen in a set of observations. Figure 4.4 shows the histogram of timeliness of the lab test ordering process.

The highest frequency of the bar graph indicates the central tendency of the data. The bold line indicates the customer specification. A customer specification indicates the least acceptable lab test ordering time. (In this example, it is two hours.) The peak of the curve shows that the average performance for lab test reporting occurs *past* the specification. Also in this example, you see most of the values in the middle and fewer tailing off in either direction. Because of its shape, some refer to it as a *bell-shaped* curve. The more technical name for it is a *Gaussian curve,* named after the German mathematician Gauss.

This type of curve shows *common cause* variation. This means that the components of variation have no undue influence on the

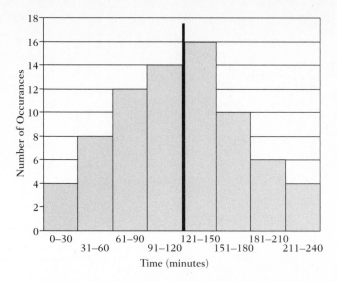

Figure 4.4   Histogram—lab test ordering time.

results. The components of variation are the machines, methods, materials, measurement, Mother Nature, and people in the process (sometimes called the 5 m's and 1 p). Typically, management blames only one of the 5 m's and 1 p when the performance of a process looks as bad as the lab reporting process. That element is the p of the 5 m's and 1 p—people. Unfortunately, this type of management often ends in disaster. What if management tells the people in this process to work faster in doing lab reports? Without finding out the root cause of the delays in lab test reporting, people in the process may just work faster and make more mistakes (affecting another customer requirement such as accuracy). They may have to redo lab reports because of mistakes and the process will take even longer as a result.

Figure 4.5 shows the second type of variation called *special cause* variation. You can see from the picture of variation that the distribution is not bell shaped. There are two peaks in the data. Therefore, one or more of the 5 m's or 1 p have had an undue influence in the process. Management should still not focus on the p since only 5 percent to 15 percent of the time special cause variation is due to the people. In manufacturing settings the predominant special cause variation is due to machines and in

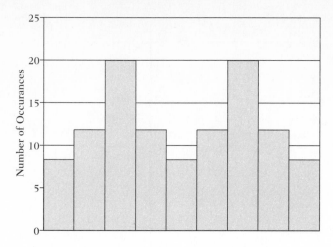

Figure 4.5 Histogram bimodal distribution.

service-related businesses the predominant special cause variation is due to methods.

Keys to Using This Tool

- Remember to have five to seven measurement cells when your database is 100 or less.
- Use histograms when you have continuous data only.
- Analyze your histogram for special cause or common cause variation.
- Don't rush to assume people are the special cause because in most cases they aren't.
- In manufacturing, first focus on the machine as the special cause.
- In service-related businesses, focus first on the methods as the special cause.
- While we recommend the histogram, box plots and normal frequency charts can do the same thing for you.

Tool #4 The Pareto Chart

We just reviewed the favored tool for analyzing data when you have collected continuous data. The other type of data teams can collect is discrete data. Discrete data is counted data—go/no-go, off/on, yes/no, and defect/no defect type data.

When the data is discrete, most teams create a Pareto chart. The Pareto chart is named after an Italian economist, Vilfredo Pareto who in the sixteenth century proved mathematically that 80 percent of the world's wealth was controlled by 20 percent of the population. This 80–20 rule eventually proved applicable in arenas other than economics. For example, 80 percent of your day is spent on 20 percent of your job description, 80 percent of your scrap is in 20 percent of your floor space, and so on.

When dealing with discrete data, the project team should create reason codes for why a defect occurs and count and categorize the data into these reason codes.

Figure 4.6 shows a grocery store example for an unduly long wait in line to check out. The grocery store project team creates reason codes as to why the wait is so long. For every time a reason code is determined, the team puts a tic mark in the appropriate place on a check sheet. After a predetermined time goes by, the team then calculates the most frequently occurring value, the next most frequently occurring value, and so on to create the Pareto chart found in Figure 4.7.

Keys to Using This Tool

- While most times the Pareto chart will be created based on the frequency of times a given event occurs, the project team should also consider making the Pareto chart based on impact. For example, if the dollar impact of an event has a greater effect on the business than the frequency of an

Item	Frequency	Comments
Price check	142	
No money	14	
No bagger	33	
Register out of tape	44	
Forget item	12	
Override	86	Manager assistance needed.
Wrong item	52	
Miscellaneous	8	

Figure 4.6 Data collection grid.

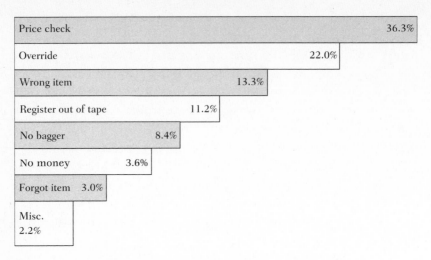

Figure 4.7 Pareto chart on data collection.

event, the Pareto chart should be made based on the dollar impact.

- Always work to reduce the highest contributor on the Pareto chart whether it is based on frequency or dollar impact. It is easier to reduce the largest problem by 50 percent than eliminate a small problem.

Tool #5 The Process Summary Worksheet

The goal of a Six Sigma project team is to improve effectiveness and efficiency. Efficiency is measured in terms of cost, time, labor, or value. The process summary worksheet is a "roll-up" of the sub-process map indicating which steps add value in the process and which steps don't add value. Moreover, each of the non-value-added steps is categorized for the type of non-value-added activity. The following are the most common types of non-value-added activities:

- *Moves:* Steps in the process where the product or service is moved from one place to another.
- *Delays:* Steps in the process where the product or service is waiting for the next step in the process.
- *Set-up:* Steps in the process that prepare the product or service for a future step.

- *Internal failures:* Steps in the process that have to be re-done.

- *External failures:* Steps in the process where a failure is detected by the customer.

- *Control/inspection:* Steps in the process where the product or service is reviewed to ensure customer satisfaction.

- *Value-enabling:* Steps in the process that technically don't add value but are necessary for the functioning of the organization.

To determine whether a step in the process adds value or not, the following three criteria must be met:

1. The customer of the step in the process must consider it important.

2. There is a physical change to the product or service.

3. It is done right the first time.

When one or more of the preceding criteria is not met, the step is considered non-value-added and that step must be categorized into one of the aforementioned types of non-value-added elements.

In Figure 4.8, you can see an example of a process summary analysis worksheet where most of the steps don't add value and over 40 percent of the non-value-added steps are due to a delay.

Process Step	1	2	3	4	5	6	Total (Minutes)	Percent
Time (minutes)	1	20	15	45	10	15	106	100
Value added	X					X	16	15.1
Non-value added		X	X	X	X		90	84.9
Internal failure			X		X		25	23.5
External failure		X					20	18.9
Control/inspection							0	0
Delay				X			45	42.5
Prep/set-up							0	0
Moves							0	0
Value-enabling							0	0

Figure 4.8   Process summary analysis worksheet.

Keys to Using This Tool

- Don't spend unnecessary time determining whether a step adds value or not. If the project team can't reach agreement whether a step adds value or not use an alternative decision making method, such as a majority vote.

- Note from Figure 4.8 that the first line of the process summary analysis worksheet indicates the amount of time it takes for the step to be completed.

- Don't list the worst case time for the step to be completed or the best time. Use an estimate of a representative time.

- If the goal of the project team is to improve cycle time of the process the percent column could be for time, not frequency, as seen in Figure 4.8.

- Once the process summary analysis worksheet has been completed, create a microproblem statement about the most frequently occurring non-value-added steps. For example, from Figure 4.8 we would create a microproblem statement such as "Why is there so much time in Step 4 (the Delay)?"

Tool #6 The Cause-Effect Diagram

We repeatedly stressed the importance of root causation in Chapter 3. The most important tool to assist the project team in determining root causation is the cause-effect diagram. This tool captures all the ideas of the project team relative to what they feel are the root causes behind the current sigma performance.

As you can see in Figure 4.9, the cause-effect diagram has the microproblem statement in a box to the far right. Extending from this box is a diagonal line with six lines attached. These six lines represent the 5Ms and 1P.

Keys to Using This Tool

- While all ideas should be captured, be careful that the team doesn't brainstorm too many ideas in the people section. Remember, people are rarely the root cause of problems in a process.

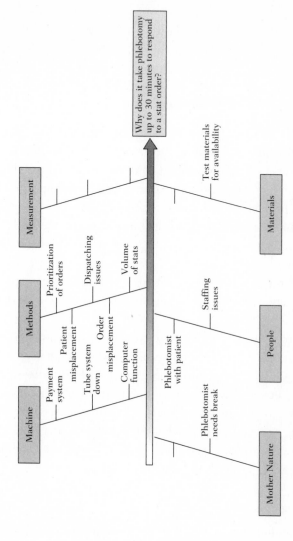

Figure 4.9 Cause-effect diagram—phlebotomy response time.

79

- Make sure to capture all ideas.

- Don't criticize or debate ideas.

- Once all ideas are captured, make sure ideas are clarified so that everyone understands one another's ideas.

- Gather duplicates together.

- Once ideas have been clarified and duplicates gathered, the team should vote on what they consider the more likely ideas.

Tool #7 The Scatter Diagram

Once ideas have been prioritized after use of the cause-effect diagram, the most important thing the project team does is validate the remaining ideas with fact and data. As we indicated in Chapter 3, the validation of root causation is one of the most important things a Six Sigma project team does.

The team can validate through one of three methods. Using basic data collection, a designed experiment, or through the scatter diagram.

The scatter diagram takes an idea about root causation and tracks corresponding data in the response the team is trying to improve.

In Figure 4.10, we see a scatter diagram that tracks frequency of communication with timeliness of lab orders. We see that most of the values go downward from left to right. This pattern shows a correlation between frequency of communication and timeliness of lab orders. This type of correlation is called a *negative* correlation. The term negative is not bad. It simply means that as communication goes up (i.e., goes from low to high), the timeliness of lab orders goes from high to low (this is desired).

Keys to Using This Tool

- Remember that correlation does not mean causation. There may be a third factor explaining the correlation. For example, there may be a relationship between ice cream sales and shark attacks but one doesn't cause the other. The third factor is seasonality.

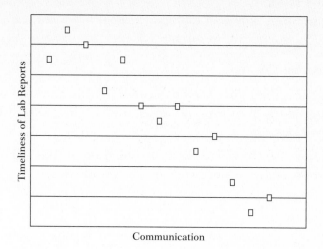

Figure 4.10   Scatter diagram – negative correlation.

- Make sure to use the scatter diagram with continuous data only.

- Make sure the two axes are corresponding so a true relationship can be determined. Make sure there is proper scaling and spacing on your diagram.

Tool #8 The Affinity Diagram

An affinity diagram is used to help sort and categorize a large number of ideas into major themes or categories. It is especially useful when the team is ready to brainstorm solutions in the Improve stage of DMAIC.

The steps in creating an affinity diagram are relatively simple. They are:

- Have each team member write one idea per Post-it note and post on a wall randomly.

- As ideas are read off for clarification, sort ideas into similar groups.

- Create a "header" card for each general category of ideas below it.

Figure 4.11 shows an example of ideas a project team brainstormed for going to a restaurant.

Keys to Using This Tool

- Follow the rules of brainstorming. This means not criticizing ideas, capturing all ideas, and making sure everyone participates.

- Don't debate where an idea should go on the affinity diagram. If two people think an idea should be in two different groups, write the idea a second time and put it in a second category.

- When creating the "header," try to reach consensus but don't try to wordsmith an idea. Try to set an environment of compromise.

- To narrow the list of solutions, multi-vote on the ideas under the header cards.

Tool #9 The Run Chart

Earlier in this chapter, we discussed the histogram and Pareto chart. Think of both of these tools as similar to a camera where a

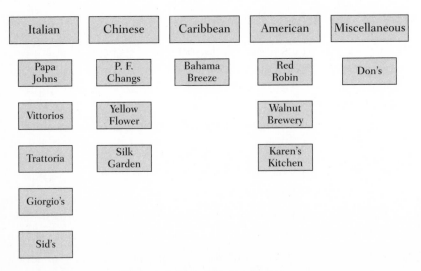

Figure 4.11   Affinity diagram.

snapshot of the process has been taken. Most people own both a camera and a camcorder, the latter of which records some event over time. Using this analogy, the run chart is similar to a camcorder, recording some process element over time.

Figure 4.12 shows an example of a run chart of someone who is tracking their weight over time. You can see that while some variation exists over time, this person's weight seems consistent and predicable over time.

Now examine the run chart in Figure 4.13. It shows after Week 9 this person started a diet.

You note a decline in weight. Technically, you can see a trend downward. The technical term *trend* applies to a process when a run chart has seven points in a row going downward or upward. A *shift* is when seven points in a row are above or below the average line on the run chart (Figure 4.14).

Keys to Using This Tool

- A run chart should be used when the project team is interested in seeing some measure over time.

- Don't interpret the chart prematurely. Too many times a project team sees one or two points going one direction and assumes this means there is a trend or shift.

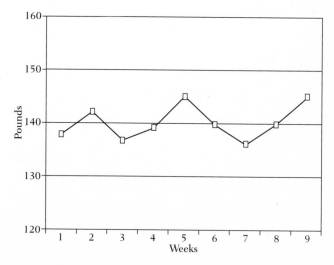

Figure 4.12 Run chart—weight over time.

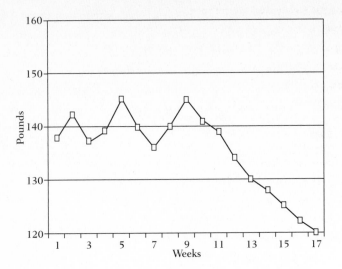

Figure 4.13　Run chart—weight over time: trend.

- In addition to examining the data on a run chart for trends or shifts, look for unusual patterns. Two points above the average line and then two points below in a repeating pattern could indicate something unusual is happening in the process.

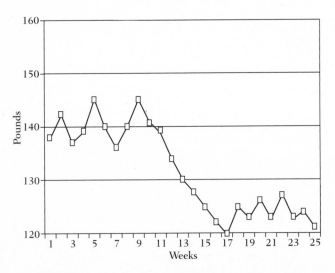

Figure 4.14　Run chart—weight over time: shift.

Tool #10 The Control Chart

Similar to a run chart, a control chart uses the data from a run chart to determine the upper and lower control limits. Control limits are the expected limits of variation above and below the average of the data. These limits are mathematically calculated and indicated by dotted lines.

In Figure 4.15, you can see a straight line, which indicates the average of the data. The upper and lower control limits indicated by the dotted lines tell the project team when the process is no longer consistent, predictable, and repeatable.

When a point "goes out of control" one or more of the 5 m's and 1 p have had an undue impact on the process (also known as *special cause* variation).

In Figure 4.15, we see a control chart for someone's diastolic blood pressure. You can see that a reading above 130 doesn't mean that the patient has suffered a stroke or heart attack but clearly the process of normal blood pressure has changed and corrective action should be taken before a more serious problem occurs.

Keys to Using This Tool

- Don't confuse control limits with specification limits. Specification limits are the least acceptable product or service in

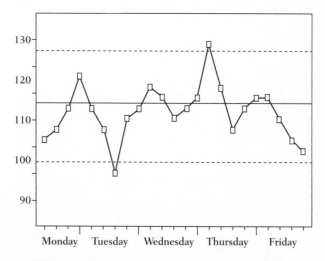

Figure 4.15 Control chart—diastolic pressure.

the eyes of the customer. The customer dictates specification limits. Control limits are the expected limits of variation that is determined by the process itself.

- Think of specification limits as the voice of the customer. Think of control limits as the voice of the process.

- Gather enough data for the 5Ms and 1P to exhibit enough variation so that the control limits are representative of the process.

- There are as many types of control charts as there are processes.

Summary

Chapter 4 addresses the 10 major technical tools a project team member uses during the time they are on a Six Sigma team. These are not the only tools a Six Sigma team may use. However, the tools covered in Chapter 4 are those that are most common for every team member to be aware of and knowledgeable about.

KEY LEARNINGS

- Every Six Sigma project team utilizes a series of tools in their work to improve sigma performance.

- The critical-to-quality (CTQ) tree helps a team identify the needs and requirements of the customer.

- A process map is a graphical display of the suppliers, inputs, process steps, outputs, and customers affecting a project team.

- There are four types of process maps. In the Define stage of DMAIC, there is the map of how the process is currently operating at the highest level. It is called the high-level process map. In the Analysis stage of DMAIC, there is the subprocess map. In the Improve stage of DMAIC, the team creates the should-be map. In Design for Six Sigma, there is the could-be map.

- The histogram is a graphical display of the number of times a given event is seen in a set of observations. Among its uses is telling the project team whether they are dealing with common or special cause variation.

- Common cause variation occurs in a process when no one of the components of variation (machines, methods, materials, measurement, mother nature, or people) has an undue influence on the process.

- Special cause variation occurs when one or more of the components of variation are having an undue influence on the process.

- The Pareto chart divides data into the vital few versus the useful many. This is based on the concept of the 80–20 rule.

- The process summary analysis worksheet separates value-added from non-value-added steps in the process. The steps are then categorized into the types of nonvalue activity.

(continued)

KEY LEARNINGS (CONTINUED)

- The most common non-value-added activities are moves, delays, set-ups, internal failures, external failures, control/inspections, and value enabling.

- The cause-effect diagram is a brainstorming tool that helps teams generate factors that affect poor sigma performance.

- The scatter diagram is a tool to assist a team in establishing a relationship between some factor and the response the team is trying to improve.

- The affinity diagram is yet another tool to assist a project team gather its thoughts. It is typically used to help a team generate ideas to improve sigma performance.

- The run chart monitors some value over time. It should be examined for shifts, trends, or unusual patterns.

- The control chart shows the expected level of variation for a process variable enabling a project team to determine when the process is no longer consistent, predictable, and repeatable.

CHAPTER 5

10 "Soft" Tools You Will Need on a Six Sigma Team

In Chapter 4, we reviewed 10 technical tools that any Six Sigma project team member is expected to use in their work of applying DMAIC. At first, these tools may present a challenge as team members both learn these tools and apply them to their actual work. After the first or second use of the tool, confidence grows in their usage.

Technical tool usage is not the only area of expertise a team member must possess. There are several tools that are considered non-technical in nature that a team member must learn. Sometimes these non-technical tools are called *soft* tools, because virtually none of them have any mathematics or statistics associated with them. While this may be good news to those on Six Sigma teams that have some degree of math phobia, in reality, these soft tools can be challenging. The challenge of the soft tools that we are about to discuss in Chapter 5 centers around the fact that so many of these tools are applied to people in the organization. Thus, it is important that Six Sigma team members learn them carefully and apply them diligently and tactfully. Without them, the chances of Six Sigma improvement reduce dramatically. With them, success is just around the corner.

The 10 tools covered in Chapter 5 can be divided into two major categories. Five of the 10 tools focus around the acceptance of the Six Sigma project team's solutions. The other five tools focus on how the team conducts its work.

The Concept of Acceptance

In our second Six Sigma book, *Making Six Sigma Last, Managing the Balance between Cultural and Technical Change,* we discussed a simple equation that contributes to the success of Six Sigma:

$$Q \times A = E$$

Q refers to the quality of the technical elements of Six Sigma, whether it be the strategic component that is the responsibility of management or the tactical elements of Six Sigma projects which is the responsibility of the Six Sigma team members. *A* in the formula refers to the acceptance of *Q* and *E* refers to the excellence of the results.

At the Six Sigma project level, acceptance refers to how well the project team's solutions are embraced by the stakeholders. Stakeholders are those individuals affected by the team's solutions or those individual's needed to implement the team's solutions.

The equation $Q \times A = E$ is a multiplicative function. This means the team should evaluate how well they have done *Q* (usually on a 1 to 10 scale where 10 is excellent and 1 is poor) and evaluate how well they have attempted to gain acceptance of their *Q* with stakeholders (again using a 1 to 10 scale). Multiplying the two numbers together will determine how successful the team will be with their project. A 60 is usually the minimum number necessary to have a successful project.

We addressed many of the tools in Chapter 4 that will assist the team in generating a high Q. We now detail the major tools necessary for a project team to generate a high *A* number.

Tool #1: The Stakeholder Analysis Chart

A stakeholder is anyone affected by the solutions of a Six Sigma project team or anyone needed to implement the solutions of a Six Sigma project team. The stakeholder analysis chart is an analysis of the key stakeholders affected by a Six Sigma project. The chart does two things: First, there is an analysis of where the key stakeholders are currently in terms of acceptance to the solutions. Second, there is the projection of where the key stakeholders need to be if the team is to be successful.

Figure 5.1 shows an example of a stakeholder analysis chart.

First, let's review what each column means. The first column is "Key Stakeholder." A key stakeholder is a stakeholder who has influence over other stakeholders. It is quite possible that a Six Sigma project team could have solutions that affect hundreds of stakeholders. It is not feasible to expect a Six Sigma project team to seek out hundreds of stakeholders to gain their acceptance. Therefore, a Six Sigma project team should identify only their key stakeholders.

Let's examine the remaining columns, starting from the far right and moving to the left. The last column indicates someone who is strongly supportive (Makes It Happen). This is someone who not only does what is asked of them by way of the project, but

Key Stakeholder	Strongly Against Having It Happen	Moderately Against Having It Happen	Lets It Happen	Helps It Happen	Makes It Happen
Robyn	O				→X
Rick	O			→X	
Hanna		O			→X
Josh		O			→X

O = current
X = needed

Figure 5.1 Stakeholder analysis chart.

also goes out of their way to do more than is asked. The column to the left (Helps It Happen) is designated for those who do what is asked of them and do it well. The next column (Lets It Happen) is designated for those who are neither for nor against the proposed solutions. They will not get in the way of the team implementing its solutions. The Moderately Against column is reserved for those who will not do what is asked of them relative to the project. Finally, to be in the Strongly Against column means not only does this stakeholder not do what is asked of them, but tries to recruit others against the solutions.

As you can see from Figure 5.1, Robyn is strongly against the project team's solutions as indicated by the "O." The "X" indicates where Robyn must be if the project team is going to be successful.

The stakeholder analysis chart is a critical first step to gaining acceptance to the project team's solutions. In keeping with the concept of Six Sigma being a management philosophy based on fact and data, a stakeholder analysis chart is a way of measuring support to the team's solutions.

Keys to Using This Tool

- Don't list every stakeholder; list only those that are key to the implementation of your solutions.

- Use actual names of key stakeholders. Don't list functions or departments (e.g., finance, manufacturing).

- To determine where the key stakeholders are currently will require data collection. That means talking to key stakeholders at a conceptual level about the project and how they will be affected.

- Recognize that to be successful in implementing a set of solutions, a key stakeholder does not necessarily need to be moved to the "Makes It Happen" column. Many times a key stakeholder only needs to be in the "Helps It Happen" or even in the "Lets It Happen" category.

- Keep the list confidential. The goal is not to "bad mouth" those that are not currently in their desired level of support.

Tool #2: Planning for Influence Chart

Figure 5.2 shows a planning for influence chart. Once the project team has identified a gap between where a key stakeholder is currently and where they need to be in order for their solutions to be implemented, a planning for influence chart needs to be created. The gap between current and desired positions usually indicates some form of resistance. There are four common types of resistance. It is the responsibility of the project team to diagnose the type of resistance, the underlying issue behind the resistance, and to develop a strategy to overcome the resistance that will move the key stakeholder to the desired state of support for the project team's solutions.

First, let's review why Robyn is resistant. The first type of resistance is called *technical resistance*. As it turns out, Robyn will

Key Stakeholder	Type of Resistance	Underlying Issue	Strategy

Figure 5.2 Planning for influence chart.

have to learn some new skills to implement the solutions of the team. These new skills are well within Robyn's capabilities, but she is resistant. What is the underlying issue behind her technical resistance? The underlying issue is feelings of inadequacy and the potential for feeling stupid. Therefore, the strategy is to educate her on the new skills she will need to use and to reassure her through information and involvement with the new solutions. Figure 5.3 shows the planning for influence chart filled out for Robyn.

In Rick's case (Figure 5.4), he is afraid that the new solutions will take away his power. This type of resistance is called *political resistance*. When a key stakeholder is exhibiting political resistance, the underlying issue is feelings of loss. The strategy for political resistance is to stress to the key stakeholder what is gained by implementing solutions even if something is lost.

In Josh's case (Figure 5.5), he is focused on control issues. He believes that the solutions are being forced on him and his

Key Stakeholder	Type of Resistance	Underlying Issue	Strategy
Robyn	Technical	Feelings of inadequacy or stupidity	Education Involvement Information

Figure 5.3 Completed planning for influence chart for Robyn.

Key Stakeholder	Type of Resistance	Underlying Issue	Strategy
Rick	Political	Loss	Stress what is gained through implementing the solutions

Figure 5.4 Completed planning for influence chart for Rick.

department. What he doesn't know (or care about at this point) is that the solutions will benefit both him and his department. Instead, he is resistant because the solutions were created without his involvement. This type of resistance is called *organizational resistance.* Since the underlying issue is around control issues, the strategy to overcome it is to have the key stakeholder take control (or even the credit if needed) for the proposed project.

Finally, there is the case of Hanna (Figure 5.6). She has just experienced several personal losses in her life, including the death of a close relative. She is resistant to any changes at work because of her emotional state. This type of individualistic resistance has little to do with the actual project. Instead, the underlying issue is one of emotional paralysis. The strategy to deal with this in the short term is to have the key stakeholder do less over a longer period of time.

Key Stakeholder	Type of Resistance	Underlying Issue	Strategy
Josh	Organizational	Control	Key stakeholder is given control or credit for the solutions

Figure 5.5   Completed planning for influence chart for Josh.

Keys to Using This Tool

- Not all resistance is created equal. Recognize that it is important to properly diagnose the type of resistance so that the proper strategy can be employed.

- Some stakeholders may exhibit more than one type of resistance. In these cases, attempt to derive the most dominant form of resistance and apply the type of strategy for the dominant form of resistance first.

- Recognize that in some cases (Technical and Political) the strategy is aimed at changing the resistor. In other cases (Organizational and Individual), the strategy is aimed at modification of the solutions.

Tool #3: The Threat/Opportunity Matrix

Six Sigma project team members will have worked on their project for months. By the time they have generated and selected their

Key Stakeholder	Type of Resistance	Underlying Issue	Strategy
Hanna	Individual	Emotional paralysis	Doing less over a longer period of time

Figure 5.6   Completed planning for influence chart for Hanna.

solutions, their commitment to them usually is highly enthusiastic. The problem with this enthusiasm is that they unrealistically think every stakeholder should share this enthusiasm even though they haven't been part of the work that has led to these solutions. Therefore, project team members must take care in creating the need for their solutions.

One tool to assist in creating the need for a project team's solutions is the threat/opportunity matrix. This matrix attempts to answer two questions for a project team. First, what will happen if they don't implement their solutions (the threats to the existing process)? Second, what will happen if they successfully implement their solutions (the opportunities to the existing process)?

A credit card company was recently trying to reduce incidences of fraud. The project team was extremely happy with four major solutions. However, some of the solutions would mean changing the way work was currently conducted. Thus, resistance could occur among some stakeholders. To overcome this resistance, the project team brainstormed answers to the two questions mentioned above.

After coming up with six answers, they determined whether these answers would occur in the first 12 months after implementation or occur after the next 12 months. If the answer occurs within the next 12 months, it is called a short-term threat or opportunity. If the answer occurs beyond the next 12 months, it is called a long-term threat or opportunity.

Figure 5.7 shows the work of the credit card fraud team's threats and opportunities. They have been placed in the appropriate quadrant of the matrix based on the determination of the team whether they are short-term or long-term threats or opportunities.

Keys to Using This Tool

- Project teams need to recognize that for any threat or opportunity, there needs to be data to support it. If you "can't prove it, don't use it."

A project team is better off with a smaller more viable list of threats or opportunities that can be supported. Teams often make the mistake of overloading a stakeholder with multiple threats or opportunities hoping "something will stick." This is a dangerous mistake. Often, when this happens, the less convincing threat or opportunity becomes the focus of discussion between a project team

Short-Term Threats	Short-Term Opportunities
• Negative impact to profitability. • Increased negative publicity to our organization.	• More time spent on pursuing new leads versus tracking bad clients. • Less job frustration.
Long-Term Threats	**Long-Term Opportunities**
• Layoffs due to not meeting business objectives.	• Greater bonus potential.

Figure 5.7   Credit card fraud team's threat/opportunity matrix.

member and a stakeholder. You are far better off when you have a shorter, more convincing list of either threats or opportunities.

Tool #4: The Pay-Off Matrix

As project teams move through the DMAIC process, the ultimate goal is to generate a set of solutions that drive sigma improvement. When the project team does a good job in Analysis, there should be a validated set of root causes that emerge. These root causes should lead to a healthy set of solutions that either reduce, soften, or eliminate the root causes. One problem that the Six Sigma project team may encounter is generating too many solutions they feel strongly about.

A simple and effective tool to help the team sort through a large number of solutions is the pay-off matrix. The pay-off matrix has two axes. The x axis is the level of impact of the solution. The two quadrants of the x axis are low-to-high impact of the solution. The y axis is ease of implementation, also rated from low to high.

The pay-off matrix is used by having the Six Sigma project team rate each solution for ease of implementation and impact to improving sigma. As can be seen in Figure 5.8, those solutions in the upper right-hand quadrant should be implemented first. Often, the

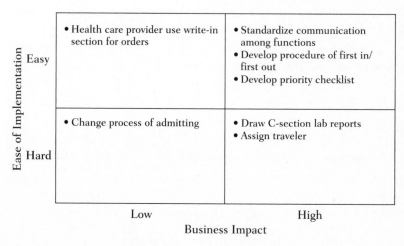

Figure 5.8 Payoff matrix.

pay-off matrix can cull a large number of solutions down to a more manageable number. The example in Figure 5.8 is taken from a health care project team trying to improve cycle time for lab testing.

Keys to Using This Tool

When used properly, the pay-off matrix cannot only prioritize solutions but possibly eliminate some solutions. For example, in the lab testing example, changing the admitting process solution in the lower left-hand quadrant is unlikely to be implemented because it is neither high impact nor easy to implement.

Be leery of teams putting everything in the upper right-hand quadrant. Not every solution is easy to implement and will have high impact toward sigma improvement.

Tool #5: The Solution Vision Statement

Another tool to help convince stakeholders of the need for a set of solutions is the solution vision statement. Simple in its concept and similar to the threat/opportunity matrix, the solution vision statement helps the team become more specific with what the new process solutions will do to those affected by the solutions.

A mistake a project team often makes is speaking in general terms or platitudes when trying to gain acceptance of solutions from stakeholders. The solution vision statement is a detailed three-column chart that forces project team members to generate specific behaviors that will be welcomed in the new process.

Figure 5.9 shows an example of a solution vision statement taken from a patient registration project.

Solution	Results	Behaviors
Modify patient registration form	Less time registering	Five lines to fill out rather than 14
Deletion of all duplicate forms	Happier customers	Less time filling out forms

Figure 5.9 Solution vision statement.

Keys to Using This Tool

- Focus on the Changed Behaviors column. When stakeholders see less work (results), they may feel that it sounds too good to be true. This skepticism can be reduced when they see the actual changed behavior associated with the solution.

- Like the threat/opportunity matrix, more is less when dealing with this tool.

The Concept of Team Dynamics

As we discussed in our third book, *Six Sigma Team Dynamics: The Elusive Key to Project Success,* the most common reason teams fail is their lack of formal focus on team dynamics. Team dynamics are the motivating and driving forces that propel a team to its goal or mission.

Most teams will be made up of individuals with diverse backgrounds and experiences. Six Sigma is aimed at transforming the business into managing with facts and data: On a project team that means taking people's ideas and validating them to improve sigma performance. Team members who have varied backgrounds and experiences will result in Six Sigma team meetings that can turn chaotic if not well managed. Our remaining tools in this chapter are aimed at helping the team leader reduce chaos and channel the team member's ideas to positive use.

Tool #6: The Team Meeting Agenda

Over the course of four to six months, a project team may meet 20 to 30 times. Sometimes these meetings will be to status other team members about work that has been done outside of the entire group. In other meetings, actual decisions are made by the entire group. In either case, meetings must be conducted in an effective and efficient way.

To assist teams in this endeavor, one of the most important tools for each meeting is an agenda.

An agenda is a work plan for each time the Six Sigma team meets. The agenda highlights what is to be accomplished, the method that will be used to accomplish the action item, who the responsible party is, and the amount of time designated for the action item to be completed.

Figure 5.10 shows an example of an actual agenda for a Six Sigma team. The Six Sigma team wants to work on their root causes. Their desired outcome is to brainstorm as large a list as possible of xs that affect Y. The method or tool that will be used is the fishbone diagram (also known as the Ishakawa diagram or cause-effect diagram). The agenda also references who is the responsible party to lead this activity and, finally, indicates the targeted time allotted for this activity. It should also state who the "time keeper" and "scribe" will be for the meeting. The time keeper manages "the clock" and the scribe is responsible for documenting all work and decisions.

Keys to Using This Tool

- A common mistake a team leader makes with the agenda is to underestimate the amount of time a given element will take to complete. Always allow proper time for a given element to be completed.

- The agenda should be reviewed by the team and agreed upon prior to its use.

- The agenda should be posted on a flip chart and be referenced through the team meeting.

- In addition to the Time Allotted column, make sure to have the Desired Outcome and Method column filled out so that the team understands both the goal of the meeting and the method to be used.

Element	Desired Outcome	Method	Responsible Party	Time Alotted
Root cause determination	Brainstorm a large list of xs that affect Y	Fishbone diagram	Black Belt and team	90 minutes

Figure 5.10 Sample Six Sigma team meeting agenda.

Tool #7: Ground Rules

While an agenda will help the team establish *what* needs to be done during a given meeting, of more importance will be *how* the team gets its work done. To that end, a Six Sigma team should establish a list of ground rules for how they will behave when they are together. These ground rules should be brainstormed and agreed to by the entire team.

Guidelines for a Six Sigma team meeting should be around how to make the meeting more effective and efficient. For example, in order for the agenda to work, the entire team should be present. Therefore, "starting on time and finishing on time" is a common ground rule for Six Sigma teams.

In addition, many times a Six Sigma team member might have preconceived notions about the project. Therefore, a good ground rule is to "keep an open mind."

These and other ideas should be brainstormed and agreed to by the Six Sigma team. Figure 5.11 shows the type of ideas that typically are listed on the ground rule flip chart.

Keys to Using This Tool

- Use a negative poll to gain agreement. A negative poll asks: "Does anyone disagree with this ground rule?" In this way, the team can gain agreement quickly for an idea and, if a team member disagrees, they can say so.

Ground Rules
- Start on time, finish on time.
- Keep an open mind.
- Decisions will be made by everyone, not the highest ranking employee.
- No cell phones.
- Keep side-bar conversations to a minimum.
- Only excused absences from the room.
- Talk to the idea, not the person.

Figure 5.11   Ground rules sample.

- Don't make a list that is too long. Most ground rule lists don't extend beyond seven or eight items.

- If there is disagreement about a ground rule, have the group discuss and attempt to gain agreement. If you can't get agreement, then don't use that ground rule.

- Always post the ground rules for each meeting.

- Make sure that everyone has the responsibility to enforce ground rules.

Tool #8: The Parking Lot

One major problem that Six Sigma project teams encounter is a team member attempting to discuss an issue that is not directly related to the agenda. Sometimes these diversions will be generated by team members who are well intended. Other times, these diversions are attempts by a team member to divert the team because they are resistant to the work of the team. In either case, it is important to redirect the team back to the work stated on the agenda.

The tool to use to make sure the team gets back on track is the *parking lot*. The parking lot is a flip chart posted in the room. When a topic not related to the agenda is raised, it is discussed by the team. If it is agreed that this is a diversion, the topic is written on the parking lot flip chart. The team resumes discussion of what is on the agenda. As the meeting is wrapped up, the team leader should then revisit the parking lot list and assign action items to handle what was put on the parking lot.

Figure 5.12 shows a parking lot example and what was decided by the team at the end of the meeting.

Parking Lot Item	Action Item at End of Meeting
Compensation issues for the team	John will address with project champion
Discussion of impact of this project in other processes	Review of data collected with other project team leaders

Figure 5.12   Sample parking lot.

Keys to Using This Tool

- Don't allow the parking lot to be used as a landfill. If the team leader ends each meeting with assigning action items associated with the parking lot issues, the entire team will see the parking lot as a viable tool to get a team back on track.

- Assign the person whose item(s) is being captured in the parking lot the action item so that there is greater likelihood that the action item will be addressed.

- Don't rush every perceived diversion to the parking lot. This will result in less participation by the entire team. Allow sufficient time for a person to discuss what is on their mind. Only raise the issue of something belonging in the parking lot when there is sufficient evidence that a diversion is occurring.

Tool #9: The Plus Delta Review of Each Team Meeting

A simple but effective tool is to have each Six Sigma team meeting end with an evaluation of that meeting. Have each team member report on their perception of what went well during the meeting (the "plusses") and what could have been done differently (the "deltas").

Figure 5.13 shows an example of a plus/delta exercise done by one Six Sigma project team.

As you can see from Figure 5.13, the plusses and deltas were brainstormed around two areas. First, the content plusses and deltas. "Content" refers to the actual work around DMAIC that the Six Sigma project team is expected to complete. Some experts call this the "What" of the project team. The second area of plusses and deltas is centered around the method of how the work is achieved. Some experts call this the "How" of the work. As can be seen from this example, the work of the team should list both the method and content plusses and deltas for each meeting.

Keys to Using This Tool

- Be careful how you phrase deltas. Deltas are things that should be done differently the next time the team meets.

Content Plusses
- Completed most of the agenda items.
- Determined root causes that explain current sigma performance.
- Steve's (Master Black Belt) presentation.

Content Deltas
- Last item on agenda was not completed. Let's allow more time for last agenda item next time.

Method Plusses
- Use of Parking lot for possible wave 2 project issue.
- Brainstorming.
- Everyone's participation.
- Use of cause-effect diagram.

Method Deltas
- Side bar conversations still going on. Let's have everyone be enforcers next meeting.

Figure 5.13   Sample plus/delta exercise.

Deltas are not negatives. Negatives are not motivating. If things didn't go well, indicate how they should be changed so that the team can be more effective and efficient. While this is a subtle difference, it is an important one.

- Always start with what went well in the meeting. While it is human nature to find fault, it is important that the team recognize what they are doing well so these activities occur in future meetings.

Tool #10: Activity Reports

Successful Six Sigma teams excel at project management. Project management refers to how well a team organizes, plans, and controls the steps in DMAIC work. Activity reports assist you and your team leader with getting work done. An activity report lists the tasks and activities needed to be done between times the team meets to learn about DMAIC. Once the task or activity is listed, the person with the primary responsibility is named, the start date and finish dates are shown, and the planned and actual date of completion for that task or activity noted.

An activity report is shown in Figure 5.14 that reflects a Six Sigma team starting their work around validation of customer requirements.

Keys to Using This Tool

- Keep the tasks and activities at an appropriate level of detail. They should be neither too detailed nor too high level.

- The primary responsible party for the task or activity should not be confused with the person actually doing the work of that activity or task. It simply is the person on the team responsible for making sure the task or activity gets done.

- It is not unusual for the start and finish dates to be the same, particularly for smaller tasks that can be done in one sitting.

- Team leaders are encouraged to review patterns in planned versus actual start and finish dates. Often, review of these reports will alert the project team leader to where there may

Task/Activity	Primary Responsibility	Start Date Planned/ Actual	Finish Date Planned/ Actual	Comments
Create survey	Team leader	March 10/	March 10/	
Have team review survey	Team	March 15/	March 18/	
Modify survey	Team leader	March 18/	March 21/	
Complete final survey	Team leader	March 19/	March 22/	
Send out survey to customers	Team member #1	March 21/	March 24/	
Verify survey receipt	Team member #2	March 25/	March 26/	
Review survey upon return	Team leader	April 7/	April 10/	
Compile survey results	Team member #1	April 14/	April 17/	

Figure 5.14   Sample activity report.

be problems with performance that the team leader will have to address.

Summary

During the course of the existence of a Six Sigma team, there is the need to use a variety of different tools and techniques. In Chapter 4, we addressed the more common technical tools.

In this chapter, we visited the "softer" tools that will be used by a Six Sigma team. These tools are sometimes referred to as "soft" tools because they tend not to be technical or mathematical. While they are described as "soft," in actuality they may present more of a challenge to a Six Sigma project team than the technical tools covered in Chapter 4. This is because while the technical tools are more complicated initially, after a time or two they can become second nature. The problem with the softer tools covered in this chapter is they are applied to people. As such, they can become complicated because of their application.

This chapter and the tools included are divided into two major areas. The first five tools are used to gain greater acceptance to the solutions generated by a Six Sigma project team. They include such tools as the stakeholder analysis chart, planning for influence strategies, and threat/opportunity matrices.

The second half of this chapter was devoted to tools that will increase team dynamics. Among the tools addressed were a vibrant team agenda, what should be included in ground rules for Six Sigma team meetings, and the use of a parking lot.

KEY LEARNINGS

- Six Sigma teams must learn not only technical tools that will improve sigma performance but tools that will help stakeholders gain greater acceptance to solutions that drive sigma improvement.

- A stakeholder analysis chart identifies key stakeholders (those affected by Six Sigma solutions or needed to implement them), their current level of support for the Six Sigma solutions, and the desired level of support in order for the team to be successful.

- A planning for influence chart indicates the source of resistance being experienced by a stakeholder, what the underlying issue is for the stakeholder, and what strategy should be employed to move the stakeholder to the desired level of support.

- To create the need for a project team's solutions, the threats and opportunities as to what will happen if the solutions are implemented (opportunities) and what will happen if the solutions are not implemented (threats) need to be created.

- The pay-off matrix is a tool that helps prioritize solutions for implementation by helping a team indicate the easiest, highest impact solutions.

- The solution vision statement helps to focus on the new behaviors that will occur once the solutions are implemented.

- Team dynamics are the motivating and driving forces that propel a team to its goal and mission.

- Agendas assist a team in becoming effective and efficient.

- A vibrant agenda includes the desired outcome, the method used to accomplish the desired outcome, the responsible party for that item on the agenda, and the allocated time for that activity. It should address the roles and responsibilities during the team meeting, including the time keeper and scribe.

(continued)

KEY LEARNINGS *(CONTINUED)*

- Ground rules help a team establish how work will be done during a Six Sigma meeting in such a way to ensure that maladaptive behavior doesn't happen.

- The parking lot captures digressions to the agenda.

- Plusses/deltas are a way to evaluate what went well in a meeting and what could be done differently the next time to improve team effectiveness and efficiency.

- Activity reports are a way for teams to capture and implement work to keep on track so that teams meet their goals in a timely manner.

CHAPTER 6

10 Common Questions about Six Sigma

Our consulting organization has been associated with Six Sigma since its inception in the 1980s. During the last 20 years, we have heard virtually every question asked about both the concept and application of this cutting edge management philosophy.

In our final chapter, we address 10 common questions asked about Six Sigma and provide our insight into their answers. It should be noted that in some cases, these questions are honest forms of curiosity about the topic. In other cases, these questions are forms of resistance on the part of the questioner. For purposes of this chapter, we assume the best-case scenario about the intentions behind each question.

Question #1   Isn't Six Sigma just like other quality initiatives in the past, almost all of which were failures?

By far, this is the most common question we hear. As we have already alluded, Six Sigma uses many of the same tools and techniques as other quality initiatives, but there are huge differences between Six Sigma and previous efforts.

First, other quality initiatives never gained the attention of top management. Whether the quality initiative was Statistical Process Control, Total Quality Management, Hoisin Planning, or other quality initiatives, it was a rarity for management to actually be involved. What typically happened was project teams were immediately formed among those that had an interest in improvement. These teams attempted to utilize quality tools and techniques, but without the support of management. Thus, the effort was half-hearted as were the results.

Six Sigma is different because of management's active involvement. Jack Welch at General Electric said that Six Sigma was the most important initiative he brought to General Electric in the 20 years he was at the helm. His successor, Jeffery Immelt, mentioned expanding Six Sigma four times in his first interview with the *Wall Street Journal*. The other two finalists for Jack Welch's succession, James McNerney and Robert Nardelli brought Six Sigma to their new organizations (3M and Home Depot, respectively) in the first month after leaving General Electric.

Why has Six Sigma garnered such support from such high-level executives? Because the executives use Six Sigma strategically, as an enabler to achieving the business objectives of the organization (see Chapter 2). With the support, encouragement, and resource allocation of management, Six Sigma has become a way of doing business in the organizations that embrace it, something that never happened with other quality initiatives. How many other quality initiatives have had the support of management like Six Sigma?

With that management support, results follow. In recent months, our consulting firm has assisted our clients generate multi-million dollar cost savings while improving customer satisfaction and improving the bottom line. One financial services client reduced dispute resolution time for a credit card process from over 38 days to less than 3. Another client, a health care provider, reduced unexpected complications and improved patient registration. If something is successful, it is used. These kinds of results attract the active involvement of management. When management supports something, it will work. Therein lies the difference between Six Sigma and other quality initiatives.

Question #2   How will I know if my organization is successfully implementing Six Sigma?

There are several signs you should be looking for if your organization is becoming successful in its efforts to implement Six Sigma.

First, management in your organization will begin to become more fact-based. Attending a meeting will result in decisions made by data rather than the person with the loudest voice. Someone in those meetings will ask to see the data, whether that data is a Pareto chart, a histogram, or a survey from a customer.

Second, you will start to become more familiar with the concept of *process*. As we described earlier in this book, a process is a series of steps or activities that takes inputs, adds value, and produces outputs for a customer. While everyone talks about being customer focused, only those that begin to measure, manage, and improve the processes of their organization will truly be customer focused. Thus, if your organization is successfully implementing Six Sigma, you and others in your organization will become more familiar with the processes you either work in or are affected by. In addition, you will become aware of the key measures of effectiveness and efficiency for those processes.

Third, you could expect to see and participate in more improvement teams. When an organization starts a Six Sigma initiative, the first teams will appear to be a novelty. After some period of time, improvement will become an expectation of every employee in the organization. Thus, the concept of improvement teams and your periodic participation on them will become standard fare rather than a novelty.

Fourth, the focus of energy of a Six Sigma organization changes. Reward and recognition migrates from the fire fighter to the arsonist catcher. What this means is that the organization you work in will become proactive rather than reactive.

Question #3   Isn't Six Sigma going to rob me of my creativity?

This question has become more prevalent since National Public Radio (NPR) ran a segment on this very topic. NPR indicated that many employees are concerned that their creativity will be limited by having to be in an organization that manages with facts and data.

Just the opposite will happen. Employees will have far greater opportunity to exhibit their creativity in a Six Sigma organization. There are two major ways that a Six Sigma culture encourages creativity rather than hampers it.

First, while on a DMAIC project team, the success or failure of the team is directly related to how well project team members tap into their creativity. Recognize that while decisions are made based on data, the team enters the root causation phase of Analysis with the responsibility to generate root causes through brainstorming. This, by definition, will cause project team members to use both their experience and creativity relative to the project. Again, in Improve, project team members must brainstorm ideas that will generate improvement in sigma performance. Time and again, I have seen that teams with great ideas (that are tested and verified) dramatically improve sigma performance.

Second, there is another tactical methodology that helps to create new processes or products. This design for Six Sigma methodology is known by its initials DMADV, which stands for Define, Measure, Analyze, Design, and Verify. DMADV is used when a process or product does not currently exist that is needed to positively impact a strategic business objective of the organization. The creativity of DMADV project team members is pivotal toward the success of its goals.

Therefore, whether the team is using DMAIC or DMADV, creativity is a must if the team is going to be successful.

Question #4   Will I lose my job if Six Sigma is successful?

One of the problems with a quality improvement approach years ago called Process Re-engineering was that virtually all of the benefits touted to management were workforce reductions.

The goal of Six Sigma is to improve both effectiveness and efficiency. Efforts that focus exclusively on efficiency (like process re-engineering) often can appear like a workforce reduction effort. When efforts like Six Sigma work on effectiveness (which you will remember is improving how well you meet your customer's needs and requirements) properly, it is typical for the business to grow and expand, not contract.

You should also remember our discussion of business process management in Chapter 2. Six Sigma should always be structured in a way to achieve the business objectives of the company. I haven't yet seen Six Sigma be exclusively devoted to just the reduction of employees engaged in inefficiency.

Having said that Six Sigma is not an employee reduction program, the following also has to be said: If your job is exclusively devoted to work around inefficiency, ultimately your job is a target for possible change or elimination. To not acknowledge this fact would be deceptive. If this is the case, you want to expand your work knowledge into other areas of the business. In the best case, as your organization improves both effectiveness and efficiency, your skills could be used elsewhere in the organization. Additionally, if your current work is focused on inefficiency, it is even more important to work on a Six Sigma team. The skills you master as part of a Six Sigma team will dramatically assist your career development, whether those skills will be used in your current position, a new position in your current organization, or some other company.

Question #5   We have tried improvement before, why should Six Sigma be any different?

Since the 1980s, many organizations have made half-hearted attempts at improving their organization through quality. I would be the first to say that whether the effort was Statistical Process Control, Total Quality Management, a Just-In-Time effort, or some other well-intentioned program, it probably failed.

Have you ever considered why it failed? I have spent considerable time and money studying why quality efforts have failed. What I and others in my organization have found is that previous efforts failed for the following reasons:

- Little or no management support and involvement.
- There was not a strategic element associated with previous efforts.
- Management of the acceptance of other initiatives never occurred.

Let's briefly discuss how Six Sigma properly addresses each of these failures. First, management historically has not been involved in quality efforts because they didn't see the connection between those quality activities and how their business was conducted. To them, quality was the domain of engineering or technical types, similar to the reputation of Information Technology. Fortunately, Six Sigma clearly defines how management becomes involved using Six Sigma as a philosophy and strategy of helping them achieve business objectives.

Second, this strategy, called Business Process Management, dictates how management will be involved with Six Sigma quality activities both during the initiation and the maintenance of the strategy of Six Sigma.

Third, if you have been a part of a quality initiative that failed, think of how well (or more likely, poorly) the acceptance of the quality effort was managed. In all likelihood, there was little or no management of the acceptance of the quality effort.

Once again, Six Sigma is different in this regard. As we discussed in the previous chapter, a series of "soft" tools are used in a Six Sigma initiative that are totally directed toward gaining acceptance to Six Sigma whether it be directed at management or an individual contributor.

Question #6   I'm not good at math. Isn't this going to be difficult for me?

I often say that if I can make my living teaching Six Sigma, anyone can learn it. I even have grade transcripts from school that prove I am not the smartest mathematician. However, the good news is that much of the math associated with Six Sigma is simple, direct, and useful.

In school, I always felt that the math was about theory. Or to put it another way, in school I felt I was learning the intricacies of how a carburetor worked but never how to drive a car. To me, the math associated with Six Sigma that you have to learn is more along the path of how to drive a car. Most of the math in Six Sigma is adding, subtracting, simple multiplication, and division.

We have worked with many Six Sigma project teams. Most project teams tell us after the completion of their project how they had dreaded the math involved but that overall the statistical calculations were the least of the problems they encountered. Between computer programs like Mini-tab and the assistance of

Master Black Belts, the math associated with project work is not as bad as they thought it would be.

Instead, project teams frequently cite other issues they struggled with much more than math. Our next series of questions deal with these more important problems.

Question #7   What do I need to know so I don't become a part of failed Six Sigma team?

Teams rarely fail because they use the wrong tool or technique. This is even more so after individuals have been part of a few teams. They quickly learn to master the concepts and tools of Six Sigma. At Eckes and Associates we have gathered data on both our successes and our failures. The data shows that the biggest problem teams face will be in dealing with the concept of team dynamics.

In our third Six Sigma book, *Six Sigma Team Dynamics: The Elusive Key to Project Success* we reviewed many of the pitfalls that teams encounter. Like so many other initiatives in life, the issue of leadership is a crucial variable in either the success or failure of a Six Sigma team.

As we indicated in *Six Sigma Team Dynamics,* leadership comes in many forms. First, executive management must create an environment where they actively and demonstratively endorse Six Sigma as their management philosophy. Without this active endorsement, Six Sigma will, at best, end up being a short-lived cost savings initiative. In addition, in Chapter 2 we discussed how management must create the Six Sigma strategy through identifying and measuring processes and ultimately picking high-profile, low-performing processes. Next, leadership manifests itself through the project Champions who sponsor and guide the project to completion.

Leadership is an important aspect of team dynamics. The project Champion will have a variety of responsibilities from before the team is formed, through the four to six months they exist as a team, and even after the team is disbanded.

However, as we discussed in our previous chapter, there are a series of "soft" tools that assist a team in creating and maintaining team dynamics. These tools fall into two major areas. Tools associated with preventing maladaptive behaviors and intervention tools to assure that maladaptive behaviors don't occur again. As stated in our previous chapter, such tools as agendas, ground rules, and setting specific roles and responsibilities for each team member are virtual guarantees for increased team dynamics. Knowing how and when to intervene when team dynamics go awry is yet another key to successful team dynamics.

Question #8 My plate is already full. How will I have the time to implement a Six Sigma initiative?

For those who are younger than 40 years of age, you may not remember the *I Love Lucy Show*. There is an episode where Lucy and her friend Ethel decide to get a job at a local candy manufacturer. They are placed on a production line where they are expected to pack individual candies into a box. The problem occurs when the production line is going too fast and they simply can't keep up with the work. Both Lucy and Ethel are well intended and trying the best they can, but this is a broken process. They are exhausted. They clearly would think their plates are full. But this also is a process in need of improvement. Yes, the responsibility for fixing this process is that of management. But smart management will enlist the support and involvement of those that live in the process to get information and ideas as to how the process can be improved.

There is considerable variation in the amount of time team members spend on a Six Sigma project. Those team members who have previous experience or current skills associated with project management spend considerably less than the average 20 percent of work time associated with Six Sigma project time. We have seen some teams spend upwards of 50 percent or more of their time on Six Sigma project work but these teams tend to be more disorganized and rarely achieve their project goals of improved sigma performance.

Someone who asks the question above apparently has developed a tolerance for the current level of ineffectiveness and inefficiency in their work. They have lived and worked in processes so broken they have come to believe that inefficiency is their work. When done properly, what falls off the plate is all the empty calories in the organization that deal with being ineffective and inefficient.

Having said this, it is also important to note that it is management's responsibility to send the clear message that process improvement is part of the job description.

Question #9   Is Six Sigma a guarantee of success? I heard Motorola is having problems with Six Sigma.

Six Sigma is not a guarantee of success in your business. Think of the analogy of preventive medicine. You can take all the precautions of eating right, exercising regularly, not smoking or drinking to excess and yet still experience illness. However, with Six Sigma as your management philosophy, the odds are that you will be sick as an organization less often and less severely.

Remember, at the highest level, Six Sigma is attempting to improve the effectiveness and efficiency of an organization. A problem many organizations encounter is the bias toward improvement of efficiency in the organization at the expense of effectiveness.

There are two major reasons for this bias toward improvement of efficiency, which is particularly acute in the first year of implementation. First, management typically is unaware of the cost associated with their current levels of ineffectiveness and inefficiency. Therefore, they are anxious to see a dramatic as possible return on their investment of outside resources, which are typically needed in the first year or two of implementation. Therefore, where does the short term cost benefits exist for quicker ROI? Clearly, it is in the current level of inefficiencies within the processes of the organization.

Second, it is much easier to quantify the costs associated with inefficiency versus improving effectiveness. What do you think is easier to measure, machine downtime or the longer term benefits of a happy customer? It is obviously the efficiency measure of machine downtime.

Ultimately, if Six Sigma is going to be a success in your organization, it needs a balance between improvement of effectiveness and efficiency. If your focus is on improving the efficiency of a process that produces Porsches and your customers desire a Chevrolet, Six Sigma will not work the way it could for you.

Question #10   Are there good consultants who will waive their fee and take a percentage of the cost savings they claim to generate for their clients?

Are there consultants who do this, yes. Are they good, no. Let's examine why.

What would you think of a surgeon who would say, "Look, I will waive my fee for doing surgery on you and you get back to me with a percentage of your earnings from me saving your life?" If I had this proposal from a surgeon I would immediately question how good he or she is. I would feel it was a marketing ploy from a less than successful surgeon trying to drum up some new business. I want a surgeon with a proven track record of competency who will charge top dollar if they are worth it. And something tells me if your life was in jeopardy, you would make the same decision.

As a Six Sigma consultant, I feel confident in my skills. But much like the surgeon, there are no guarantees. Data we accumulated over the years indicate there is an 80 percent likelihood of either a dramatic shift in your culture or at least generating a significant ROI. For example, in recent years, our client base has been generating anywhere from a 2 to 1 to a 20 to 1 ROI for their first year Six Sigma implementation efforts.

Having said all this, our data still indicates 20 percent of our clients have failed to generate ROI. A consultant should not be responsible for lackluster effort, not paying attention to consultant advice, or populating project teams with the equivalent of the roster of a bad baseball team.

Summary

This chapter has addressed some of the more common questions asked about Six Sigma and provided answers. As we indicated, many of these questions are asked honestly. Other times they are forms of resistance. We have attempted to answer them from the perspective of the honest inquirer.

KEY LEARNINGS

- Six Sigma is different from other quality initiatives in that it has generated significant management involvement.

- Signs that an organization is embracing Six Sigma include more management with fact and data, management of process versus function, participation on project teams, and a change in the reward and recognition system.

- The creativity of employees is utilized more in a Six Sigma culture, not less.

- While your job may change, it is unlikely Six Sigma will reduce the workforce in your organization. It is far more likely that jobs will be lost if your company doesn't do anything about their current level of ineffectiveness and inefficiency.

- Previous efforts at improvement have probably failed in your organization because of the lack of management support, no strategy related to its implementation, and lack of management of the acceptance of change.

- The math associated with Six Sigma is addition, subtraction, multiplication, and division.

- Those that have developed a high tolerance for inefficiency or think their work is mastering inefficiency will think of Six Sigma as more work.

- Six Sigma is not a guarantee of success, just a way to reduce the chance of failure for your organization.

- When you hire a Six Sigma consultant, don't look for someone touting gimmicks. Hire the best.

APPENDIX

Process Capability and Sigma Conversion Table

Capability Index (Cpk)	Process Sigma Short Term	Process Sigma Long Term	Yield	Defects per 1,000,000	Defects per 100,000	Defects per 10,000	Defects per 1,000	Defects per 100
2	6	4.5	99.99966	3	0.34	0.034	0.0034	0.00034
1.97	5.9	4.4	99.99946	5	0.54	0.054	0.0054	0.00054
1.93	5.8	4.3	99.99915	9	0.85	0.085	0.0085	0.00085
1.9	5.7	4.2	99.9987	13	1.34	0.134	0.0134	0.00134
1.87	5.6	4.1	99.9979	21	2.1	0.207	0.021	0.0021
1.83	5.5	4	99.9968	32	3.2	0.32	0.032	0.0032
1.8	5.4	3.9	99.995	48	4.8	0.48	0.048	0.0048
1.77	5.3	3.8	99.993	72	7.2	0.72	0.072	0.0072
1.73	5.2	3.7	99.989	108	10.8	0.08	0.11	0.011
1.7	5.1	3.6	99.984	159	15.9	1.6	0.16	0.016
1.67	5	3.5	99.98	233	23.3	2.3	0.23	0.023
1.63	4.9	3.4	99.97	337	33.7	3.4	0.34	0.034
1.6	4.8	3.3	99.95	483	48.3	4.8	0.48	0.048
1.57	4.7	3.2	99.93	687	68.7	6.9	0.69	0.069
1.53	4.6	3.1	99.90	968	97	10	0.97	0.097
1.5	4.5	3	99.87	1,350	135	13	1.3	0.13
1.47	4.4	2.9	99.81	1,866	187	19	1.9	0.19
1.43	4.3	2.8	99.74	2,555	256	26	2.6	0.26
1.4	4.2	2.7	99.65	3,467	347	35	3.5	0.35
1.37	4.1	2.6	99.5	4,661	466	47	4.7	0.47
1.33	4	2.5	99.4	6,210	621	62	6.2	0.62
1.3	3.9	2.4	99.2	8,198	820	82	8.2	0.82
1.27	3.8	2.3	98.9	10,724	1,072	107	11	1.1
1.23	3.7	2.2	98.6	13,903	1,390	139	14	1.4
1.2	3.6	2.1	98.2	17,864	1,786	179	18	1.8
1.17	3.5	2	97.7	22,750	2,275	228	23	2.3

1.13	3.4	1.9	97.1	28,716	2,872	287	29	2.9
1.1	3.3	1.8	96.4	35,930	3,593	359	36	3.6
1.07	3.2	1.7	95.5	44,565	4,457	446	45	4.5
1.03	3.1	1.6	94.5	54,799	5,480	548	55	5.5
1	3	1.5	93.3	66,807	6,681	668	67	6.7
0.97	2.9	1.4	91.9	80,757	8,076	808	81	8.1
0.93	2.8	1.3	90.3	96,801	9,680	968	97	9.7
0.9	2.7	1.2	88.5	115,070	11,507	1,151	115	12
0.87	2.6	1.1	86.4	135,666	13,567	1,357	136	14
0.83	2.5	1	84.1	158,655	15,866	1,587	159	16
0.8	2.4	0.9	81.6	184,060	18,406	1,841	184	18
0.77	2.3	0.8	78.8	211,855	21,186	2,119	212	21
0.73	2.2	0.7	75.8	241,964	24,196	2,420	242	24
0.7	2.1	0.6	72.6	274,253	27,425	2,743	274	27
0.67	2	0.5	69.1	308,538	30,854	3,085	309	31
0.63	1.9	0.4	65.5	344,578	34,458	3,446	345	34
0.6	1.8	0.3	61.8	382,089	38,209	3,821	382	38
0.57	1.7	0.2	57.9	420,740	42,074	4,207	421	42
0.53	1.6	0.1	54.0	460,172	46,017	4,602	460	46
0.5	1.5	0	50.0	500,000	50,000	5,000	500	50
0.47	1.4	−0.1	46.0	539,828	53,983	5,398	540	54
0.43	1.3	−0.2	42.1	579,260	57,926	5,793	579	58
0.4	1.2	−0.3	38.2	617,911	61,791	6,179	618	62
0.37	1.1	−0.4	34.5	655,422	65,542	6,554	655	66
0.33	1	−0.5	30.9	691,462	69,146	6,915	691	69

(continued)

Capability Index (Cpk)	Process Sigma Short Term	Process Sigma Long Term	Yield	Defects per 1,000,000	Defects per 100,000	Defects per 10,000	Defects per 1,000	Defects per 100
0.30	0.9	-0.6	27.4	725,747	72,575	7,257	726	73
0.27	0.8	-0.7	24.2	758,036	75,804	7,580	758	76
0.23	0.7	-0.8	21.2	788,145	78,814	7,881	788	79
0.20	0.6	-0.9	18.4	815,940	81,594	8,159	816	82
0.17	0.5	-1	15.9	841,345	84,134	8,413	841	84
0.13	0.4	-1.1	13.6	864,334	86,433	8,643	864	86
0.10	0.3	-1.2	11.5	884,930	88,493	8,849	885	88
0.07	0.2	-1.3	9.7	903,199	90,320	9,032	903	90
0.03	0.1	-1.4	8.1	919,243	91,924	9,192	919	92
0.00	0	-1.5	6.7	933,193	93,319	9,332	933	93

Index

#6 team meeting agenda, 101–102

#7 ground rules, 103–104

#8 parking lot, 104–105

#9 plus/delta review of team meeting, 105–106

#10 activity reports, 106–108

Solution vision statement, 100–101

Sony, 9

Special cause process (nonrandom), 48

Special cause variation, 73–74, 85

Stakeholder analysis chart, 92–92, 108

Statistical process control, 5

Steps of root cause analysis:
close step, 58–60
narrow step, 55, 58
open step, 54–55

Steps of Six Sigma, 29–64

Straight from the Gut (Welch), 9

Subprocess mapping, 49–50

T

Team dynamics, concept of, 101–108

Team meeting agenda, 101–102

Technical resistance, 93–94

Technical tools, 67–86

#1 critical to quality (CTQ) tree, 67–69

#2 process map, 69–72

#3 histogram, 72–74

#4 Pareto chart, 74–76

#5 process summary worksheet, 76–78

#6 cause-effect diagram, 78–80

#7 scatter diagram, 80–81

#8 affinity diagram, 81–82

#9 run chart, 82–84

#10 control chart, 85–86

Threat opportunity matrix, 96–99, 108

Tollgates:
analysis, 42–60
control, 61–64
define, 30–36
improve, 60–61
measure, 36–42

W

Welch, Jack, 8, 9

Wall Street Journal, 10